Praise for

ADVENTURES IN VEGGIELAND

"You never know—the fun of this might even encourage [your child] to try other colorful veggies later!" —*PARENTS* magazine

"Children will enjoy the full-color pictures of young people in the kitchen, and parents will discover fresh ideas for meals with even the pickiest eaters."
—*LIBRARY JOURNAL*

"Potock has developed a year's worth of family-friendly recipes along with practical, proven strategies for helping kids learn to become more adventurous eaters."
—*PUBLISHERS WEEKLY*

"This delightful book will help children—and parents—approach vegetables in a spirit of fun and exploration, instead of with the usual pressure and dread. Both the activities (Asparagus 'Log Cabins'!) and the recipes (Grilled Cabbage Brains!) are so fun, no kid will be able to resist playing with her food."
—**JENNA HELWIG,** senior food editor at *Parents* magazine
and author of *Real Baby Food*

"I ADORE this book! Melanie understands that to help children develop healthy eating habits, food has to be *fun*. These truly inspired ideas (so much more than just recipes!) encourage children to play with their food and get them tasting—and loving—everything from beets to cauliflower to broccoli."
—**JULIE CLARK,** creator of Baby Einstein and WeeSchool

"This book is a gift. Parents, children, and therapists alike will benefit from the joy and creativity these strategies bring to helping kids learn about healthy whole food."
—**KRISI BRACKETT, MS, SLP-CCC,** speech pathologist, feeding specialist,
and codirector of the Pediatric Feeding Team at UNC Health Care

"With the growing number of picky eaters, I am so grateful to have such a well-thought-out book to recommend to my clients!"

—**JILL CASTLE, MS, RDN,** childhood nutrition expert,
registered dietitian, and coauthor of *Fearless Feeding*

"Fun just explodes from every page of *Adventures in Veggieland*. Melanie Potock has created a one-of-a-kind cookbook that opens the door to a world where food is not only delicious and healthy, but also the basis of many joyful family memories."

—**NIMALI FERNANDO, MD, MPH,** founder of the Doctor Yum Project
and coauthor with Melanie Potock of *Raising a Healthy, Happy Eater*

"As a feeding therapist, I need parent- and child-friendly resources. . . . This book brings together explanations and activities that are easy to do in treatment and at home in just three easy steps: Expose, Explore, and Expand. Melanie has hit another one out of the park!"   —**DIANE BAHR, CCC-SLP,** international expert on
feeding, motor speech, and mouth function

"What a wonderful new resource! Melanie Potock's *Adventures in Veggieland* is destined to become a staple for parents and caregivers, as well as SLPs, OTs, and other professionals. With wonderful photos, clear explanations, and approachable recipes that support child participation, this book offers so many ways to explore, experience, cook, and even play with seasonable vegetables. It will change how kids eat their veggies—it has changed how I want to eat mine!"

—**LYNN ADAMS, PHD,** author of *Parenting on the Autism Spectrum*

"As a nutritionist, I know that filling our plates with vegetables is one of the best things we can do for our health, but as a mom of a reformed picky eater I also know that getting kids to eat their veggies is not always easy. *Adventures in Veggieland* takes the power struggles that never work and replaces them with fun games, yummy recipes, and a sense of adventure—I mean, what's not to love about turning beets into french fries, cupcakes, and even tattoos?"

—**SARA VANCE,** nutritionist and author of *The Perfect Metabolism Plan*

ADVENTURES
in
VEGGIELAND

Also by Melanie Potock

Responsive Feeding

Raising a Healthy, Happy Eater
(coauthor with Nimali Fernando)

ADVENTURES
in
VEGGIELAND

Help Your Kids Learn to Love Vegetables
with 100 Easy Activities and Recipes

MELANIE POTOCK, MA, CCC-SLP

THE EXPERIMENT

NEW YORK

The Experiment, LLC
220 East 23rd Street, Suite 600
New York, NY 10010-4658
theexperimentpublishing.com

This book contains the opinions and ideas of its author. It is intended to provide helpful and informative material on the subjects addressed in the book. It is sold with the understanding that the author and publisher are not engaged in rendering medical, health, or any other kind of personal professional services in the book. The author and publisher specifically disclaim all responsibility for any liability, loss, or risk—personal or otherwise—that is incurred as a consequence, directly or indirectly, of the use and application of any of the contents of this book.

THE EXPERIMENT and its colophon are registered trademarks of The Experiment, LLC. Many of the designations used by manufacturers and sellers to distinguish their products are claimed as trademarks. Where those designations appear in this book and The Experiment was aware of a trademark claim, the designations have been capitalized.

The Experiment's books are available at special discounts when purchased in bulk for premiums and sales promotions as well as for fundraising or educational use. For details, contact us at info@theexperimentpublishing.com.

The Library of Congress has cataloged an earlier edition as follows:

Names: Potock, Melanie, author.
Title: Adventures in veggieland : help your kids learn to love vegetables with 100 easy activities and recipes / Melanie Potock.
Description: New York : Experiment, [2017]
Identifiers: LCCN 2017021341| ISBN 9781615194063 (pbk.) | ISBN 9781615194179 (ebook)
Subjects: LCSH: Cooking (Vegetables) | Children--Nutrition. | Vegetarian cooking--Juvenile literature. | LCGFT: Cookbooks.
Classification: LCC TX801 .P69 2017 | DDC 641.6/5--dc23
LC record available at https://lccn.loc.gov/2017021341

ISBN 979-8-89303-079-2
Ebook ISBN 978-1-61519-417-9

Cover and text design by Sarah Smith
Cover photographs by Eric Harvey Brown, except Sweet Potato Toast by Sarah Smith

Manufactured in China

Originally published in a different binding February 2018
First printing of this edition February 2025
10 9 8 7 6 5 4 3 2 1

This book is dedicated to four people who have taught me the meaning of family and the importance of connecting around the family table:

To my dad. I can't remember a single summer growing up where we didn't have a garden, with corn taller than your six-foot, five-inch frame, and where we'd harvest kohlrabi, radishes, and sugar snap peas on a trellis. We rarely missed a sit-down family dinner except to break the rules and eat on TV trays on Sunday nights just to watch *The Ed Sullivan Show*. You taught me the importance of establishing family traditions around the joy of food, making sure we had plenty of crab feasts, weekly oyster shucking, and extra olives for every martini (personally my favorite). You always delighted in the suggestion of "just a little cookie or two" or getting together with family to celebrate anything over ice cream. The memory of you will always brighten my day, and I was so fortunate to be your "darling daughter."

To my husband, Bob, the love of my life for over forty years. You introduced me to Polish food, to warm doughnuts straight out of the oven at midnight in Little Italy, and to true love. Plus you can load a dishwasher like no other man I know, and that comes in handy when your wife is writing a cookbook.

To my daughters, Mallory and Carly, who make every holiday dinner feel like they never left home, despite being all grown-up and living on their own. There is nothing better than exploring new restaurants with you, indulging in gluten-free cupcakes, and beaming together over the array of fruits and vegetables at the farmer's market. My heart is always with you, no matter how many miles separate us . . . until we come back together once more to laugh over a family dinner.

CONTENTS

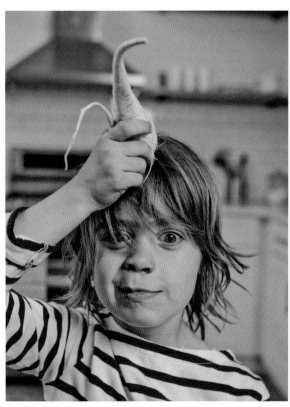

PREFACE

Play is the answer to how anything new comes about.

—JEAN PIAGET

I KNOW IT'S NOT ALWAYS easy to raise kids to be healthy, happy eaters, because I'm a mom whose first child was quite the adventurous little foodie and whose second daughter was very hesitant about new foods. In fact, during her toddler years, she ate Cheerios and milk almost every night for dinner. Today my eldest daughter, Mallory, will still eat almost anything, unless it has mayonnaise. We are still working on that. Carly, the youngest, no longer depends on cereal and milk, eats all sorts of vegetables, and is gradually accepting the fact that salsa has cilantro in it. It's going to be a long road to make friends with cilantro.

Everyone's food adventure is unique, with different roadblocks and detours. But there are three proven strategies for helping kids learn to love any kind of food, especially vegetables. I call this magic formula the "Three *E*'s"—expose, explore, expand!

First, research shows that it's vital to *expose* kids to new vegetables throughout the year. A key part of that exposure is food play. In *Adventures in Veggieland*, you'll introduce every single vegetable to your child with hands-on activities that familiarize the body and brain with the sensory aspects of fresh vegetables, including touch, aroma, and even the sound of the crunch. Think of it as a first playdate. We want it to go well, be focused on fun, and have the kids asking, "When can we get together again?"

Second, you'll begin to *explore* other aspects of that same vegetable (things like texture, taste, and temperature) via two delectable but oh-so-easy recipes. Kids prep and cook the food right along with you, every step of the way. This is where you'll introduce taste testing. Keep a jar of tiny tasting spoons on the kitchen counter, just like professional chefs do. Encourage frequent tastes of whatever you're making together. Kids need to know that not everything will taste good right away, and that's OK. Our job as chefs is to determine what else it needs to taste just right. How will we know if we don't stop and taste as we cook? Between you and me, those frequent tastings are the secret to this stage. When you have a child who will taste almost anything, and you continue to expose them to that taste over time, they learn to love that food.

Third, you'll have two more recipes showcasing that vegetable and begin to *expand* your child's palate. More complex flavors will be introduced, and the final recipe will always be a sweet treat. It won't necessarily be what you might think of as dessert, but nevertheless, it will be sweet and delicious. Sometimes the vegetables in the treats won't be obvious, but if your child is part of the process, she will know that a lot of red beets went into those delectable chocolate cupcakes. It's not about hiding vegetables—it's about including veggies whenever possible.

When we include vegetables in entrées, side dishes, and even desserts, our kids experience repeated, positive exposures. They get to explore all the sensory aspects of each one and begin to expand their variety over time.

How do I know this? It's not just my experience with my own fussy eater; it's my experience with *thousands* of picky eaters. I'm a pediatric speech language pathologist and feeding specialist, but the kids I work with just call me "Coach Mel." I'm their food coach, and together we learn to become adventurous eaters. I've helped parents raise healthy, happy eaters for over twenty years, and I'm delighted to help you on this journey. It won't happen overnight, but we will get there. Always remember to keep the adventure joyful, focus on the process (not the bite), and create wonderful memories as you parent in the kitchen.

Coach Mel

INTRODUCTION

How to use this book

Where do I start?

First, answer this question: What season is it? Turn to that chapter and that's your personal starting point. You'll find that the winter, spring, summer, and autumn chapters each highlight five seasonal vegetables. You'll learn strategies to expose children to the unique sensory aspects of that vegetable via crafts, cooking, and science, and you're on your way.

How about an example?

In the winter chapter, the first food you will encounter is beets. They feel rough and are often encrusted with garden dirt, until we wash and prepare them for mealtime. The subtle and sweet aroma drifts through the air as we peel the beets of various colors and have fun making temporary tattoos with beet juice. We'll learn how to clean off our stained fingers with a surprising tip from top chefs—but you'll have to read that chapter to learn the secret! Later in the week, or whenever you're ready, we'll begin to explore the taste and texture of fresh beets with two very different recipes to ensure that your child experiences the flavor in different ways. Later on, we'll begin to expand our palate with a beet recipe that's more adventurous, with an unexpected twist. Finally, we'll top off our beet adventure with a sweet treat that incorporates this colorful veggie into a yummy dessert. Be sure to include your child in the entire process, from washing to prepping, chopping, helping to push the buttons on the food processor, and even decorating the plate for a lovely presentation.

You have just used the Three *E*'s: You've exposed your child's entire sensory system to beets, introducing new aromas, tastes, and textures via food exploration, plus you've expanded his diet to include tasting five new beet recipes. Will he absolutely love beets at the end of this? Yes, possibly, and at the very least he'll have made friends with beets and be just fine with them coming to dinner.

Be amazed as your child experiences the joy of new foods and proud as his confidence grows while your family ventures through each chapter! You'll discover that he's more willing to interact with and taste a variety of new foods, including vegetables. That's the goal: a child who is adventurous and willing to try almost any new food, especially the healthy ones.

But it sounds like a lot of work!

Each recipe is designed to be quick yet interactive, so that you and your kids have a good time in the process. As you continue through each season, return to some of the recipes, make them again with your child, and keep presenting the vegetable in a variety of ways. The key to kids accepting and loving new vegetables is frequent exposure in a positive, fun, and experiential manner. It's about building familiarity. That's how we all learn to love new foods over time. Spending a bit of time in the kitchen with your kids, a few times a week, has incredible benefits for you and for your child.

Seriously, what's the payoff?

The facts speak for themselves. Your child may grow to be healthier and smarter and make safer decisions in his teen years. Research shows many benefits from teaching kids to prepare healthy food and eat adventurously, as shown in the following pages.

The Science Behind Expose

Over twenty-five years ago, when I was trying to encourage my own very picky toddler to try vegetables, I never knew I'd be developing a system to help other parents in the same boat! I had not heard of the science behind exposure to new foods and the importance of gardening, cooking, and playing in food together and did not embark on my career as a feeding specialist until many years later. As I watched my toddler's anxiety rise every time I presented something new on her plate, two things became very clear to me: (1) This was going to take time, and (2) I had better make it enjoyable—for both of us! It wasn't until I was in graduate school many years later that I became interested in pediatric feeding and began to pore over the science that shows how to raise healthy, happy eaters. My instincts were right.

Let's get down to the basics first: How many servings of vegetables should a child eat each day?

According to the Academy of Nutrition and Dietetics, kids need two to three servings of veggies per day—but the size of a "serving" will be different depending on whether the child is a toddler, a preschooler, or elementary age. Some guidelines offer serving sizes based on cups, but since vegetables come in all shapes and sizes, it can be hard to figure out what a "cup" means.

The following easy visual might help you remember how big each serving should be: Picture a large egg—that's a volume of about ¼ cup. Picture a tennis ball   that's 1 cup. Now imagine the recommended serving sizes for children of different ages in terms of eggs and tennis balls:

- Toddlers get 2 to 3 large eggs of vegetables per day
- Preschoolers get 2 to 3 *half* tennis balls of vegetables per day
- Elementary school kids get 2 to 3 *whole* tennis balls of vegetables per day

Just picture your kid with either an egg, a tennis ball cut in half, or a whole tennis ball in his hand. That's his serving of vegetables, two to three times each day!

Overexposure to Fast Food

Sadly, nine out of ten children in the United States don't eat enough vegetables, according to the Centers for Disease Control and Prevention, and of the "veggies" that kids do like to eat, french fries and chips were the most popular.[1] This may be due to the fact that almost one third of kids in the United States eat fast food on any given day and the default vegetable (despite other options) served with fast food is a potato product—typically french fries or chips. For 29 to 38 percent of children, fast food is a main source of food.[2]

But don't all kids love fast food—and is it really that big of a deal? Yes—and yes, because kids are eating more fast food than ever, much more than twenty years ago. Children who eat fast food consume more saturated fat, more total fat, more carbohydrates, and more added sugars. They consume less fiber and more calories overall. In fact, kids will eat more calories throughout the day *because* of that fast-food meal, in addition to the many calories *in* the meal. Research shows that eating fast food causes kids (and anyone) to crave the salty, fatty comfort of foods like french fries throughout the entire day.[3]

Poor nutritional health may lead to poor brain health, and kids' academic test scores seem to reflect that outcome. In a study published in the monthly journal *Clinical Pediatrics*, researchers showed that fifth graders who ate fast food on a weekly basis had lower improvements in test scores in reading, math, and science by the time they reached eighth grade. One in five of those students reported eating four fast-food meals over the course of the week, and two thirds of the fifth-graders ate fast food at least once per week.[4]

What makes fast-food-style french fries, nuggets, and burgers so appealing? Exposure! The big fast-food chains market their foods to our kids on billboards, on television, in movies, and on social media. Our preschoolers see, on average, three fast-food ads per day, and our teenagers see five fast-food ads per day. "We're programmed to seek sweet and salty foods, and fast food knows how to pander to those cravings," says pediatrician Steven Pont, who serves as medical director of the Texas Center for the Prevention and Treatment of Childhood Obesity at the Dell Children's Medical Center.[5]

Parenting Strategies for Exposing Your Child to Healthy Foods

In our book *Raising a Healthy, Happy Eater*, pediatrician Nimali Fernando and I describe seven parenting principles that offer strategies for parents to limit their child's exposures to unhealthy food—including fast food. Our seven principles can also be applied to increasing a child's exposure to healthy vegetables:

1 Parent Compassionately and Say No. Offer an alternative to the french fries from the drive-through by saying no compassionately: "I love salty fries, too, but how about we bake those pretty red beet fries from Coach Mel's cookbook tonight? They are extra healthy and yummy and we can have the fun of making them together! We can make some paper pockets to put them in and you can decorate each one. I bet Daddy would like a dinosaur on his. You are really good at drawing dinosaurs."

2 Parent Mindfully and Say No. Provide an explanation and create a teachable moment. You might say, "No, I don't buy chicken nuggets from the drive-through because they have so many preservatives in them. If you'd like me to buy some for your science fair project, and see what happens to them if we let them sit on a plate for a week—or a month—then let's do that. You can do the same with one of our homemade nuggets and compare the two. I think you might just win the science fair with that project!"

3 Parent Proactively and Say No. Try your best to pack healthy snacks or meals so that food from the drive-through isn't the only solution. Consider packing two meals at the beginning of each week that can be grabbed quickly, just in case you have to run out the door and didn't get a chance to prepare anything that day. Many of the recipes in *Adventures in Veggieland* include leftovers, which create opportunities to expose kids to vegetables once again.

4 Parent Consistently and Say No. Lay ground rules early so you don't have to say no as often. Perhaps you'd like to have some fast food on occasion. You might say, "I don't think fast food is very healthy, but sometimes it's our only option. The rule is, if neither one of us can think of how to buy a healthier meal, then we'll get fast food. But our compromise is that we'll pick one healthy option on that fast-food menu, like apple slices with our kids' meal."

5 Parent Joyfully and Say Yes! Celebrate with a small treat from the drive-through, to occasionally enjoy those foods that you don't want to include as a dinnertime habit. Eating a small ice cream cone or sharing a small order of fries every once in a while is fine!

6 Parent Bravely and Say No. Make a shopping list and don't be afraid to stick to it! Include easy, time-saving options such as precut veggies, containers of hummus, cups of guacamole, or other conveniently packaged healthy options. Keep those in a special bin in your refrigerator so you can pack a lunch-on-the-go and don't give in. You can do it!

7 Parent Patiently and Say No. Take the time to teach your kids how to spot unhealthy foods and also to spot which options at the drive-through might be healthier choices. Nutritional information is often posted on the wall of fast-food restaurants or it can be accessed on your phone via the website. Take a minute, be patient, and give the kids choices rather than always choosing the same fast-food meal.

Sometimes the big marketing machine and the influence of the outside world can feel overwhelming when we are trying so hard to raise healthy eaters. Rest assured that plenty of research has been focused on how to help kids love vegetables, and it always comes down to these same parenting principles, especially the idea of parenting consistently. Research shows that most caregivers offer a new food to a child only three to five times before giving up and concluding that the child simply doesn't like it, but the same research indicated that in fact it takes eight to fifteen exposures to successfully foster the acceptance of a new food.[6] A handful of exposures that took place randomly over the course of a few weeks simply doesn't offer enough consistency. Some kids will just tolerate the food even after fifteen exposures, and it may take even more interaction to learn to eat it with joy and enthusiasm. Becoming an adventurous eater is always going to take experience over a long period of time. It's called adventurous eating because it's a journey and an adventure, where kids encounter new foods as they grow!

The Science Behind Explore and Expand

Kids often need positive practice, over time, to become familiar with all the sensory properties of a food before they are willing to taste that food. When parents consistently offer the opportunity to play with food and to help with food-related activities like gardening and cooking, kids get those important repeated exposures. In the January 2015 issue of the journal *Appetite*, psychologists described their findings about the importance of repeated exposures to new foods, especially vegetables. When toddlers (ages one to three) in a nursery school setting engaged in sensory food play every day for four weeks, astonishing changes occurred. Not only did the little ones touch and taste more of the vegetables they explored during those four weeks, they also interacted with other new foods besides the veggies. Researchers noted that when toddlers were offered two foods, a vegetable that they had played with multiple times plus a vegetable they had not been exposed to, they engaged with the familiar vegetable first. They had a solid friendship in place with that

vegetable because they had explored it many, many times. The kids also tasted more of the exposed vegetables than the unfamiliar vegetables.[7]

Hands-on Exploration

Studies show that kids with tactile sensitivities may have picky eating habits. In another 2015 study published in *Appetite*, kids ages four to ten were asked to feel different tactile stimuli and taste different foods. Results showed a significant positive correlation between interacting with textures and willingness to taste.[8] The takeaway here is that when kids are given the opportunity to just play in food textures and get messy, it is time well spent. They are not avoiding putting the food in their mouths; they are preparing to take that first taste by exploring the food with their other senses. The activities and recipes in this book are designed for experiencing food away from the mealtime table as well as at meals themselves. The more kids experience vegetables throughout the day, the more likely they are to eat them during family mealtimes.[9] In fact, when it comes to exposing kids to vegetables, even visual exposure in the form of drawings and photos of vegetables can increase a child's willingness to taste new foods, especially for toddlers. The phrase "We feast with our eyes" may start with the simplest form: looking at food in picture books.[10]

Hands-on activities with unfamiliar vegetables can enhance a child's willingness to taste those vegetables, but the next step is to bridge the gap between tasting and getting kids to eat enough to meet the recommended daily requirement—from 1 to 2½ cups per day. Modeling your own enjoyment of vegetables and offering children tiny taste experiences so they can develop their own appreciation for those tastes will eventually turn yuck into yum.[11] Throughout *Adventures in Veggieland*, you will find tips on how to encourage kids to take tiny tastes in a playful way. Continue this approach consistently, over time, and step-by-step your child will learn not only to eat their veggies but also to enjoy them![12]

The key is in keeping it fun. When kids enjoy the process, that leads to enjoying the tasting. And remember to enjoy the process yourself! Studies show that just presenting a new food with a smile on your face increases the likelihood that your child will taste it.[13] Caregivers who, out of desperation, pressure a child to taste-test will increase the likelihood of picky eating. Taking it slowly may feel especially challenging if you are worried about your child's nutritional health. Keep in mind that the change in your child may begin with the change in the expression on your face.[14] Smile and have fun! Parent joyfully!

Parents, remember to taste-test along with your child. If you don't love vegetables, your kids are not going to love them, either. A study in *Ecology of Food and Nutrition* showed that taste testing increases the likelihood that you'll learn to love more vegetables, and that in turn is associated with your kids being willing to try more veggies. It's a chain reaction, and your positive attitude sparks the process![15]

When it comes time for serving and enjoying what you've cooked together, research from Texas A&M University showed that the types of other foods on the plate will influence the likelihood that your child will taste the new foods. Your kids are more likely to eat the new vegetable dish when it's paired with another food that is not a highly preferred food. In short, don't serve a new veggie dish with chicken nuggets if nuggets are your child's favorite food. Be sure there is something at dinner that will fill your child's belly, but offer something that's not his first choice for dinner.[16]

Rewards May Encourage Picky Eating
Parents may find themselves faltering during the transition from exposure to

exploration, where kids are encouraged to take tiny tastes. It's so tempting to incorporate a little bribery to make it easier on everyone! If we reward our kids for eating our veggies, wouldn't that make this process go must faster? What about commonly used phrases such as "Eat your vegetables and you'll get dessert" or "Eat your broccoli and you'll get a sticker"? Bribing a child with dessert implies that the vegetables are a "yucky" food that we must eat in order to get the "yummy" food. Putting dessert on a pedestal and needing it at every meal to encourage eating healthier foods is counterproductive. An enticement such as a sticker can persuade children to eat vegetables without sending the wrong message, but it seems that praise can be equally effective as a reward: A 2011 study in the journal *Appetite* suggested that nonfood tangible rewards (e.g., stickers) and nontangible rewards (praise or attention) were both effective in encouraging children to taste vegetables. Three months after the rewards stopped, the two groups were both eating their vegetables.[17]

Before you're convinced that bribery with stickers is a terrific solution, however, consider that the study did not take into account the fallout from bribery. When we bribe our children, they become expert negotiators and lose a bit of respect for the adult in charge, exerting their own power to make the grown-up give a little bit more each time when expected to do something new. Although bribery may encourage repeated exposure to veggies, the psychological environment is less than positive. When using the Three *E*'s to present new foods, keep the atmosphere relaxed and fun. Children's brains are quite malleable, and they compare new food experiences to past food experiences. Think of your child's brain as being like a filing cabinet, where you are gradually replacing negative food experiences with fresh, positive ones. The goal is to create new files of positive memories. Praise itself is rewarding, but what's even more rewarding for children is your attention.

The Three *E*'s Outside of the Kitchen

You'll discover another benefit of cooking together when you step outside of the kitchen. The connection you've made with your child while you're whisking, chopping, baking, and creating new dishes together spills over to other parts of the day, especially at mealtimes.

A 2016 position statement published by the American College of Pediatricians pointed out that, since the 1980s, "family time at the dinner table and family conversation in general has declined by more than 30%. Families with children under age 18 report having family dinners three to four times per week. One third of families with 11- to 18-year-olds eat one or two meals a week at most together. Only one fourth eat seven or more family meals per week." In studies cited by the ACP, parents reported struggling to create a space in their busy days for family meals, but most placed a high value on making family meals a priority. For many, the importance of family mealtimes ranked even higher than going on vacation together![18]

Whether parenting in or out of the kitchen, parent mindfully. Be present. Connect with your kids. Paying attention to your kids—listening, being mindful—does more than raise healthy eaters. You'll raise kids who have solid values and cherish the concept of family. Family mealtime provides consistent opportunities to reconnect in our busy lives, share values and ideas, and more.

Studies show that eating a family dinner together just five times a week has an incredible impact on teenagers. When compared to teens who had family dinners two or fewer times per week, the families eating together five times per week raised teens who were more likely to get better grades (40 percent got As and Bs) and make better life decisions around drug use and peer relationships.

In fact, those kids were 42 percent less likely to drink alcohol, 59 percent less likely to smoke cigarettes, and 66 percent less likely to try marijuana. There are undeniable benefits of sharing three or more family mealtimes per week: Kids are 25 percent more likely to eat healthy foods and 35 percent less likely to develop an eating disorder.[19] Even more striking? Almost two thirds of those teens felt that eating dinner with their own parents on a regular basis was "very or fairly important." When we make family mealtimes a priority for our kids, it's likely that they will do the same with their kids, because it was important to them. That's a legacy to be proud of! If dinner just isn't possible, don't rule out a breakfast, a picnic, a face-to-face conversation at a restaurant. It's not the table where you sit; it's who is sitting at the table that's most important.[20]

Younger children reap benefits from family mealtimes, too. Research has demonstrated that a routine that includes family mealtimes plays a crucial role in language development for children. Both expressive and receptive language skills improve when children are part of the mealtime table with their parents and older siblings, and those mealtime conversations also seem to influence early reading skills, as measured by improvement in reading scores.[21]

Along with family mealtimes, other valuable opportunities to incorporate the Three *E*'s include gardening, shopping at farmer's markets, and cooking. Once you begin to foster this love for vegetables, try gardening, too. One study demonstrated that children who participated in gardening projects scored higher in science achievement than those who did not.[22] It doesn't have to be a large garden plot. A pot of herbs or a tomato plant on the windowsill is a terrific start! Furthermore, kids who dig and plant have improved moods, better learning experiences, and decreased anxiety. So dig in the garden and get dirty!

Studies show that when kids grow their own vegetables, they are much more likely to eat them.[23] For instance, reporting on research from Saint Louis University in 2007, the science news website *Science Daily* offered the following summary: "Researchers interviewed about 1,600 parents of preschool-aged children who live in rural southeast Missouri. They found that preschool children who were almost always served homegrown fruits and vegetables were more than twice as likely to eat five servings a day than those who rarely or never ate homegrown produce."[24]

Farmer's markets likewise offer a myriad of opportunities to explore new vegetables! As parents shop, children can ask questions about new vegetables, creating a teachable moment. Children can also take part in choosing what to eat by picking out the vegetables they would like to try.[25]

Clearly, parenting in or out of the kitchen isn't simply about nutrition, grocery shopping, or digging in soil. Although research proves that the frequency of shared family meals is significantly related to our children's nutritional health,[26] spending time together and nurturing the love for healthy food affects the whole child—brain, body, and soul.

Where will you decide to start to gain exposure to new vegetables? Winter, spring, summer, autumn, or perhaps with a vegetable that you've already got in the kitchen? No matter where you begin, you're on your way to a lifetime of exploring healthy eating for both you and your children.

Part One

WINTER VEGETABLES

When people refer to "winter vegetables," most often they're referring to crops that store well, like sturdy squash and root veggies including beets, parsnips, sweet potatoes, and turnips. You may find that these crops begin to appear at farmer's markets and grocery stores as early as September, but the winter season is when you'll find a surplus of all kinds of squash and the latest variety of brightly hued cauliflower. Surprisingly, many winter vegetables benefit from being touched by frost in the winter! The cooler temperature brings out the sweetness and enhances the flavor. Now is the time to visit a farmer's field, where kids can pull their own winter vegetables straight out of the ground. The more opportunities your child has to experience "farm to table" winter vegetables, the better!

BEETS

Nothing is as sweet as a beet. Of all the nutritious vegetables, beets contain the most natural sweetness and are, not surprisingly, a favorite among kids. The dark red beetroot is found in abundance this time of year, but seek out other colors including golden yellow, pure white, and even the pink-and-white candy-striped variety. The red or yellow pigments in beets contain antioxidants that keep our liver healthy and help create new red blood cells. Try beets raw (sliced thin with a touch of lemon juice and a sprinkle of sea salt), roasted, grilled, or pickled. The greens make a scrumptious salad when torn and tossed with other greens, such as collards and kale, or try the recipe for Simply Beetiful Greens Sauté (page 20)!

EXPOSE

Beet Tattoos

Beets come in a variety of colors and, fortunately, can temporarily stain your skin yellow, red, pink, and purple. Yes, it's a good thing! Kids need to explore foods in a fun way before they consider tasting them. Temporary tattoos are sure to be a hit with kids of all ages.

What you'll need:

- Fresh beets
- Kid-safe knife (see page 259 for suggested products)
- Mini cookie cutters in simple shapes, like a heart or diamond (optional)

What to do:

❶ KIDS: Wash any dirt from the beets under running water.

❷ PARENTS: Boil about an inch (2.5 cm) of water in a shallow pan. Slice off the root ends of the beets. Place the beets upright in the water with the greens sticking upward. Boil gently on medium-high for 4 to 6 minutes, until the bottoms are fork-tender. Remove from the water and wait until the beets are cool enough for kids to handle.

❸ KIDS: Press a cookie cutter into one of the beet halves and then remove it, leaving an imprint of the shape.

❹ PARENTS AND OLDER KIDS: Cut away the beet around the shape to leave a raised "stamp" for the tattoo. Or create your own shape by whittling away at the beet!

❺ KIDS: Lick the stamp, press onto skin, and let dry. The pattern will be faint on the skin at first, but if you hold still and let it dry (it takes about a minute) you'll have a lovely light-pink tattoo!

❻ PARENTS AND KIDS: Be creative! How about putting the stamp to use for a little face painting? It all comes off in the bathtub or with a secret vegetable that magically erases beet stains (see Tip).

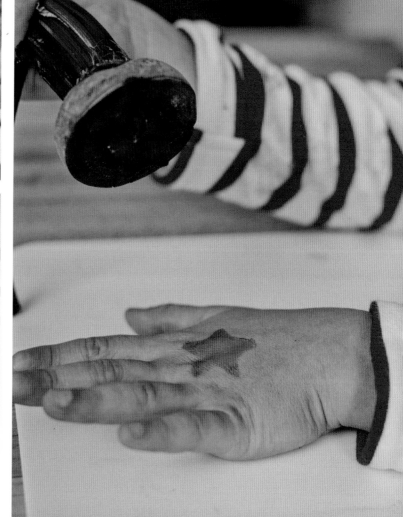

Use a piece of raw potato under running water as a magic eraser to rub off beet juice. Another cleanup trick is to gently rub the beet stains with a paste of lemon juice and sugar and rinse.

But don't be surprised if the kids decide to lick the lemon sugar off, getting a taste of sweet beets along with the "lemonade."

How your child benefits

You just helped your kid lick and smell beets, without ever mentioning eating them. If they took a crunch in the process, that's a bonus. Most importantly at this stage, they had a good time being with you—and with beets, too!

Can't Be Beet Dip

TOTAL TIME: 10 minutes (not including beet roasting time) **PREP:** 5 minutes **SERVES:** 4 to 6

Whether you're feeding a baby or a teenager, dipping is the best way to introduce small tastes of a new food, especially if your child is a hesitant eater. This quick beet dip brings out the natural sweetness of the beets, and the gorgeous color is ideal paired with crisp apple slices. Got a strict carb lover at home? Start with dipping a cracker, providing the crunch that many kids crave, then progress to the crunch of apples over time.

1 medium beet, peeled and roasted (see Tip), or 2 or 3 small packaged cooked beets

1 medium banana

2 tablespoons plain yogurt (or slightly more if your preference is a thinner dip)

1 tablespoon honey

Toss all the ingredients in a blender and blend into a sweet creamy dip! Add a touch more yogurt if you feel like the dip is too thick.

All Kids Can . . .

- Put ingredients in the blender
- Turn the blender on and off

Plus, Big Kids Can . . .

- Help peel the cooled roasted beets (or cut open the package)
- Pour the dip into a bowl

> ⤙ TIP ⤚

Roast a few beets to use in recipes for the week! Preheat the oven to 375°F (190°C). Before washing, slice off the greens and place them in a plastic bag. The greens will keep in the refrigerator for up to three days if you wait to wash them. Wash the beets, dry with a paper towel, and coat lightly with oil before wrapping them individually in aluminum foil. Place them in a small metal pan to prevent them from rolling. Roast for 45 minutes, or until cooked through. Let cool for 15 minutes before removing the foil and peeling. The peel will slide right off, like magic!

PARENTING IN THE KITCHEN

The first step to cooking is washing hands thoroughly! The Centers for Disease Control and Prevention recommend singing "Happy Birthday" *twice* to allow enough time to remove and rinse away germs. Afterward, be sure to dry hands with a *clean* cloth towel or a fresh paper towel. Establishing a familiar hand-washing routine sets the stage for kids to know what's coming up next: cooking!

Rosy Red Fries

TOTAL TIME: 35 to 45 minutes PREP: 10 minutes COOK: 25 to 35 minutes SERVES: 4

As a pediatric feeding therapist, I can confirm one food that even fussy eaters love: the french fry. Problem is, it's not the healthiest choice. Why do kids love fries so much? Salty is a taste that is easy to detect on the tongue and very common in processed snack foods. Combine that with what some consider to be the sixth taste—fat—and it's a match made in heaven. When the foods on kid's menus have the same salty and fatty combination as processed snacks, kids find comfort because it is recognizable. The fat makes the food melt in your mouth—you barely have to chew! (Just the thought of it makes my mouth water!) Parent compassionately by teaching kids how to roast nutritious beet fries, so you can offer a healthier alternative that provides the same meltable, salty flavor.

4 large fresh beets
Olive oil to coat
Sea salt to taste

① Preheat the oven to 375°F (190°C).

② Remove the beet greens before washing. (Save them for Simply Beetiful Greens, page 20. See the storage tip on page 17.) Wash and peel each beet, using a sharp paring knife. Discard the outer peel. Cut the beets into slices, then into long, thin pieces, about the width of a pencil.

③ Place the beets on a baking sheet (lined with foil for easy cleanup, if desired) and toss with olive oil, just barely enough to coat, and sprinkle with salt. Arrange the beets on the baking sheet with enough space between each one for even roasting.

④ Roast for 25 to 35 minutes, flipping the beets halfway through the cooking time. The beets are done when they have a slight crisp to the edge.

All Kids Can . . .

- Wash and dry the beets
- Line the baking sheet with foil
- Toss the fries in olive oil
- Spread the fries on the pan

- Cut the beet slices into fries (with adult supervision) using a cat paw (see page 65)

PARENTING IN THE KITCHEN

Parents can build on the familiarity of preferred food, like fries, by making one change at a time until kids are eating all different kinds of vegetable fries. Start with the beet fries recipe, and a few days later, try changing another aspect of the taste by coating fries in coconut, hazelnut, or avocado oil. This same recipe can be used with carrots, parsnips, or sweet potatoes. Try changing up the spices: You might use a dash of sugar and cinnamon on carrots or sweet potatoes or put rosemary and sea salt on parsnips. There is no wrong combination, and it's a fantastic way to help your kids concoct different flavor combos of their own. What's more, these healthy fries will be baked with just a little oil, instead of deep-fried, and lightly salted so that everyone can indulge in the deliciousness as often as they'd like.

Simply Beetiful Greens Sauté

TOTAL TIME: 15 minutes **PREP:** 10 minutes **COOK:** 2 to 4 minutes **SERVES:** 4

Don't throw away those luscious greens when you prepare beets! They are high in calcium, iron, folate, and other crucial nutrients. Sautéing beet greens is super quick and like magic—kids can see the greens soften and brighten up in the pan right before their eyes.

3 large bunches beet greens
1 tablespoon olive oil
2 tablespoons finely chopped crystallized ginger
1 tablespoon finely chopped garlic
1 tablespoon apple cider vinegar
Salt and black pepper to taste

1 Rinse the greens and pat them dry with paper towels to soak up all the moisture. Remove the stems and chop them into 1-inch (2.5 cm) pieces. Chop or tear the leaves into bite-size pieces.

2 Place a large skillet over medium heat. Once it is warm, add the oil and allow that to warm. Now add the pieces of beet green stem, ginger, and garlic. Sauté these until they are slightly softened. Add the leaves, turning them over with a wooden spoon or tongs to ensure that they are evenly coated with the seasonings. Stir in the vinegar (it will smell amazing!) and season with salt and pepper. Continue to cook for 2 to 4 minutes, until slightly wilted and delicious!

All Kids Can . . .

- Rinse and dry the greens
- Tear or chop the leaves with a kid-safe knife
- Add salt and pepper to taste

Plus, Big Kids Can . . .

- Add the greens and seasonings to the skillet and sauté (with adult supervision)

TIP

This recipe can be adapted for any savory greens, such as Swiss chard, kale, collards, or mustard greens.

PARENTING IN THE KITCHEN

Sometimes, we need to focus on today's accomplishments, no matter how small they seem. Perhaps today your child decorated a serving platter with lovely sautéed greens and felt proud of that but didn't venture to taste this time. That's still terrific! When kids are actively engaged in cooking new recipes, they are much more likely to take a taste because they have some ownership in the process, but it won't happen every day. Thank goodness you didn't throw away those greens, because you just boosted your kid's confidence and self-esteem instead.

A Sweet Treat: Choco-Beet Cupcakes

TOTAL TIME: 45 minutes PREP: 20 minutes COOK: 18 to 25 minutes MAKES: 18 to 24 cupcakes

Just the process of cooking can lead to exploring new tastes. That's why we like to lick batter off the spoon. There is no raw egg in this batter, so go ahead and give it a lick! For another fun tasting experience, add a surprise treat while you're making these cupcakes: a rosy smoothie shot! After you puree the beets, don't wash out the blender jar, which is coated with "good-for-yous" that should never go down the drain. Just throw in ¼ cup (25 g) frozen berries (blueberries are my favorite!) and a splash of orange juice and blend.

8 to 9 ounces (227 to 255 g) packaged cooked beets or 1 large roasted beet (see Tip on page 17)
1 cup (240 ml) 2 percent milk or unsweetened vanilla almond milk
1 teaspoon apple cider vinegar
1 cup (125 g) plus 1 heaping tablespoon all-purpose flour (gluten-free if needed)
½ cup (50 g) unsweetened cocoa powder
1 teaspoon baking soda
½ teaspoon baking powder (gluten-free if needed)
⅛ teaspoon salt
¾ cup (150 g) sugar
¼ cup (60 ml) melted (not hot) coconut oil
2 teaspoons pure vanilla extract
¼ cup (45 g) dark chocolate chips
Whipped cream (for the final touch), from a can or homemade (page 68)

1 Preheat the oven to 375°F (190°C).

2 Place the beets in a blender and pulverize to your heart's content. Measure out ½ cup (110 g) of the resulting beet puree and set it aside to use in the cupcakes.

3 Pour the almond milk into a small bowl and whisk in the vinegar. While giving the milk 5 to 10 minutes to curdle slightly, line two muffin pans with paper liners and sift the flour, cocoa powder, baking soda, baking powder, and salt together in a separate bowl.

❹ Add the sugar, oil, vanilla, and pureed beets to the curdled almond milk and beat with an electric beater until it's foamy.

❺ Gently and slowly add the sifted dry ingredients to the wet ingredients and continue to beat the cupcake mix until it is smooth. Stir in the chocolate chips, except for two—eat those.

❻ Pour the cupcake batter into the muffin liners, filling each halfway. Bake for 18 to 25 minutes on the center rack of the oven, until a toothpick inserted into two spots in a cupcake comes out clean, ensuring that any wetness isn't just melted chocolate chips.

❼ Remove the cupcakes from the pan and cool on a cooling rack.

❽ Top each cupcake with a swirl (or dollop) of whipped cream (to keep it lower in sugar), or add a dollop of the Cream Cheese Frosting on page 212.

All Kids Can . . .

- Put the ingredients in the blender
- Turn the blender on and off
- Whisk the almond milk and vinegar together
- Line the muffin pans with paper liners
- Help sift the dry ingredients
- Help pour the batter into the muffin pan liners
- Add the whipped cream topping

Plus, Big Kids Can . . .

- Slice the beets (with adult supervision), using a cat paw (see page 65)
- Use the electric beater (with adult supervision)

KITCHEN SCIENCE

Ewww! Why curdled milk? When we combine the acidity of the milk with the alkaline properties of the baking soda, we create bubbles of carbon dioxide. Those little bubbles plump up the batter as it cooks, making airy, springy cupcakes!

PARENTING IN THE KITCHEN

Does your child have trouble digesting gluten? I've included a gluten-free option in most of the recipes in this book because food intolerances or food allergies can inhibit food exploration. In the case of many picky eaters, poor gut health is the culprit. When a child's body is sensitive to certain proteins, like gluten, it causes inflammation and gastric discomfort. Kids learn that eating doesn't feel good and develop a distrust of new foods.

BUTTERNUT SQUASH

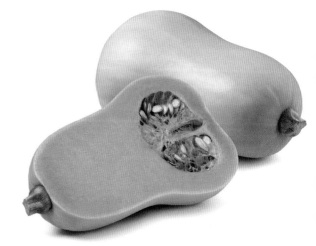

Winter squash have a distinctive hard skin to protect the flesh from the elements as it matures on the vine. Butternuts taste just like their name— buttery and nutty! They also squash the bad guy— inflammation—with the ace of antioxidants, vitamin A (which comes from the beta-carotene)! In fact, you'll get over half of the vitamin A you need each day from just a cup of squash. When purchasing butternuts at the grocery store, ask if it has already been cured. It's not absolutely necessary, but curing hardens the skin more so that it can be stored for up to six months. There are several easy methods on the Internet to cure your own squash straight from your garden or from a farm stand. Cured or uncured, store butternuts in a cool, dark place, like a pantry or cabinet.

EXPOSE

"Guess That Fruit or Veggie" Game

I need to confess that for years I thought butternut squash was a vegetable. From a strictly botanical perspective, it's a fruit, because it contains seeds. Ditto for tomatoes, cucumbers, and even pumpkins. These are less sweet than what we usually consider to be fruits, such as oranges or peaches, which may be why they are often called vegetables in a culinary context.

What you'll need:

- 6 large bowls
- 3 different vegetables ("fruits") that have seeds (be sure to include butternut or other varieties of winter squash), cubed if too large to fit under the bowls
- 3 different vegetables that don't have seeds, cubed if too large to fit under the bowls

What to do:

1 PARENTS: Hide three fruits and three vegetables under large bowls on the counter. Start with the first bowl and move on to the others one by one as kids guess correctly.

2 KIDS: Each player can ask one question about the hidden fruit or vegetable. If there are several players, each player takes a turn to ask one question before another round.

3 PARENTS: If a player guesses what's under the bowl, award her with that fruit or vegetable. The player with the most food in front of her wins!

> **TIP**

Cleaning out the seeds and pulp of winter squashes (such as pumpkin and butternut) can cause itching and irritation to the skin. For that reason, I don't recommend playing with winter squashes in the same manner that I recommend playing with food in some of the other recipes in this book. Some cooks wear rubber gloves when seeding winter squashes, while others have no reaction at all and can clean them with bare hands. At the very least be sure to wash hands and wrists with gentle soap and water after seeding, chopping, or handling the interior seeds and pulp. Kids often have sensitive skin, and you want to be careful to keep every cooking experience a positive one.

How your child benefits

In this game, not only are you teaching food science, but your kids are also practicing language concepts such as describing attributes and differences, developing social skills like turn taking and good sportsmanship, and implementing cognitive reasoning and memory skills.

Butternut Squash Risotto with Bacon and Sage

TOTAL TIME: 50 minutes **PREP:** 15 minutes **COOK:** 35 minutes
MAKES: 4 large entrée servings or 8 smaller side dishes

When kids make risotto, they will be learning the art of patience. Risotto needs to be stirred while it's on the stove for 15 minutes or more, so this recipe is best for kids ages five and up, and kids at the stove should have direct adult supervision. Younger children can add ingredients to the risotto and help you stir, so that they still play a part in creating the dish. Be prepared for a lovely aroma that will lure the entire family into the kitchen.

1 pound (455 g) packaged fresh butternut squash cubes or 1 small butternut squash, peeled, seeded, and cubed

2 tablespoons olive oil

Salt and black pepper to taste

4 cups (960 ml) chicken or vegetable broth

3 slices applewood-smoked bacon, chopped into bite-size pieces

¾ cup (115 g) chopped red onion

1 tablespoon unsalted butter

1 cup (195 g) Arborio rice

½ cup (120 ml) dry white wine (see Kitchen Science) or white grape juice (add 1 tablespoon lemon juice if using grape juice)

2 tablespoons fresh sage, cut into ribbons (or "chiffonade"; see Tip)

1 cup (100 g) freshly grated Parmesan

① Preheat the oven to 400°F (200°C). Toss the squash cubes with the oil and salt and pepper on a baking sheet (lined with foil for easy cleanup). Spread the cubes evenly on the baking sheet, being sure to leave space between each cube for even roasting.

② Roast until very tender, about 30 minutes. If you'd like a little bit more "toast" on the edges, simply turn the oven to broil for just a few minutes. Watch carefully so as not to burn them!

3 While the squash is in the oven, heat the broth in a small covered saucepan and simmer until needed.

4 In a Dutch oven or similar heavy-bottomed pan, cook the bacon and onions over medium heat until the onions are softened in the bacon grease and the bacon has a light crisp on the edges. Melt in the butter. Add the rice, stirring to coat the grains. Add the wine, stirring for 2 minutes to loosen the bits of bacon and onion that may be stuck to the bottom (deglazing the pan).

5 Add two ladles of broth to the rice, continuing to stir until the broth is absorbed with only a slight dampness at the bottom of the pan. Immediately add two more ladles and continue to simmer and stir, until almost dry. Then repeat.

Taste-test when the rice begins to look creamy in texture. It should be al dente, just like a perfect piece of pasta, which typically takes about 15 minutes.

6 Gently stir in the sage, roasted squash, and half of the Parmesan. Keep the remaining half of the cheese for sprinkling on top of each serving. Serve warm as an entrée or side dish. This is major comfort food—so relax and enjoy.

TIP

Top chefs get fancy and make little ribbons (chiffonade) with sage and leafy herbs. Pick the leaves off the stems. Stack the leaves on top of each other, roll them up tightly, and snip with scissors. With each snip, tiny ribbons will unravel and the aroma is released, bringing each dish alive with flavor!

All Kids Can . . .

- Line the baking sheet with foil
- Toss the squash cubes with the olive oil and seasonings
- Stir the risotto (with an adult's help)
- Sprinkle cheese on each serving after putting it on a plate

Plus, Big Kids Can . . .

- Cook bacon and onions (with adult supervision; bacon grease spatters easily, so consider using a splatter screen or mesh cover)
- Pour the broth into a pot and heat

KITCHEN SCIENCE

Why cook with wine? Wine is often called for in recipes as a way to enhance flavors, but parents sometimes worry about whether it's OK to use wine when cooking with kids. Because risotto is cooked at a higher heat over an extended period, the alcohol content diminishes, but the subtle acidity and flavor remain. Some alcohol may still remain in the risotto and would vary with portion sizes. If you prefer not to use wine in your dishes, substitute white grape juice and add a touch of acidity with a splash of lemon juice.

Balsamic-Roasted Butternut Squash Moons

TOTAL TIME: 45 minutes **PREP:** 15 minutes **COOK:** 20 to 30 minutes **SERVES:** 6 to 8

Kids love shapes, all kinds of shapes, especially moons! As you slice up the butternut squash to prep it for roasting in this recipe, the slices will resemble different moon-phase shapes. The end piece will create full moons, the center pieces (where the seeds lie) will be crescent moons, and the neck of the squash will look just like a first-quarter moon, when half of the moon's disc is illuminated in the sky. Teach even the youngest kids these lunar concepts and spark their interest in the science of stargazing. Be sure to ask what moon they'd like on their dinner plate: full, crescent, or first quarter?

1 large butternut squash
¼ cup (60 ml) balsamic vinegar
3 tablespoons olive oil
3 tablespoons honey
1 tablespoon chopped fresh rosemary (optional)
Salt and black pepper to taste

❶ Preheat the oven to 450°F (230°C). Line a rimmed baking sheet with parchment paper (it's more nonstick than foil).

❷ Wash the outside of the butternut squash. Before slicing in half to remove the seeds, cut across the "butt" end of the squash, creating solid "full moons" ¼ inch (6 mm) thick for roasting.

❸ Cut the rest of the squash in half and remove the seeds and pulp. Slice across the halves to create crescent moons ¼ inch (6 mm) thick and across the neck to create first-quarter moons, also ¼ inch (6 mm) thick. You can cut the peel off now or wait till they're roasted, when the peel comes right off the moon.

❹ Arrange the squash moons flat on the baking sheet.

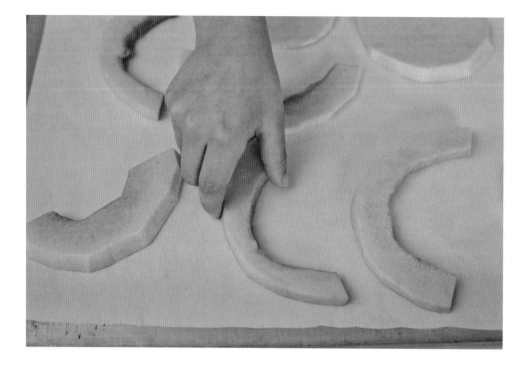

⑤ Whisk the vinegar, oil, and honey together and lightly drizzle half of this dressing over the moons. Sprinkle with rosemary (if using) and salt and pepper. Flip each moon, drizzle with dressing, and season again. You may have some dressing left over.

⑥ Roast the squash until all the pieces are fork-tender and the dressing is caramelized. (For more about caramelization, see page 195.) If one side appears to be browning, flip each moon over to achieve even color and caramelization. Roasting typically takes 20 to 30 minutes.

All Kids Can . . .

- Line the baking sheet
- Wash and dry the outside of the squash
- Help scoop out the squash seeds and pulp
- Arrange squash pieces on the baking sheet
- Whisk oil and vinegar and drizzle it over the moons
- Sprinkle seasoning over the moons

Roasted Butternut Squash Salad with Glazed Pecans

TOTAL TIME: 50 minutes PREP: 20 minutes COOK: 30 minutes SERVES: 4 to 6

The key to introducing kids to any mixed green salad is to keep it simple by adding just two or three simple ingredients to the greens and sticking with a mild, clear dressing. This salad fits the bill with just greens, cubes of roasted and cooled butternut squash, and crunchy glazed pecans, all lightly tossed in a simple yet delicious vinaigrette. Toss some pomegranate seeds (arils) on top to tempt the taste buds.

12 ounces (340 g) packaged fresh butternut squash cubes or 1 small butternut squash, peeled, seeded, and cubed

3 tablespoons coconut oil, melted

Salt and black pepper to taste

1 tablespoon light brown sugar

1 tablespoon water

¼ teaspoon pure vanilla extract

½ cup (60 g) raw pecan halves

3 cups (about 90 g) lettuce (spring mix or chopped butter lettuce is ideal)

Pomegranate seeds

HOMEMADE DRESSING

3 tablespoons olive oil

2 tablespoons Champagne vinegar

1 teaspoon Dijon mustard

Salt and black pepper to taste

1 Preheat the oven to 400°F (200°C). Toss the squash cubes with the coconut oil and salt and pepper on a baking sheet (lined with foil for easy cleanup), leaving space between the cubes for even roasting.

2 Roast the squash for 25 to 30 minutes, until the cubes are tender and browned on the edges. Remove the cubes from the pan and allow them to cool slightly.

③ While the squash is roasting, toast and glaze the pecans. Make the glaze by mixing the brown sugar, water, and vanilla, stirring them together until the sugar is dissolved.

④ Heat a saucepan over medium heat (use a pan just big enough to hold the pecans in a single layer) and when the bottom is warm, add the pecans. Toast for 2 to 3 minutes, stirring occasionally. Stir in the brown sugar mixture and heat until the liquid is dissolved, leaving a glaze on the nuts. Place the nuts on parchment paper or a clean plate to cool. Do not touch the pecans until they have cooled—the glaze is very hot!

⑤ To make the Homemade Dressing, combine all the ingredients in a small jar. Screw the lid on tightly. Wrap a few rubber bands around the glass jar to provide added grip. Parents, hand your kid the jar and tell them to shake it until the dressing has emulsified—that is, the oil and vinegar are completely mixed. Then tell them to keep shaking the jar. Inspect and tell them to shake it again. Continue until the child has worked up an appetite.

⑥ Chop the glazed pecans. Toss the lettuce, squash, and pecans with the Homemade Dressing, just enough to coat lightly. Sprinkle the pomegranate seeds on top and serve.

All Kids Can . . .

- Line the baking sheet with foil
- Toss squash cubes in the oil and seasonings
- Spread the squash on the baking sheet
- Mix the glaze for the pecans
- Chop the cooled pecans with a kid-safe knife
- Put the dressing ingredients in a jar and shake!
- Toss the salad
- Sprinkle the pomegranate seeds on top

PARENTING IN THE KITCHEN

For hesitant eaters, deconstruct the salad into small samples of squash, chopped pecans, lettuce, and pomegranate seeds, along with a small sample of dressing for dipping. Add one more sample of the constructed salad, where all the ingredients are mixed together with dressing. Use this technique whenever you meet resistance to unfamiliar combinations, to build confidence in your kids as they learn to adjust to the mixture of new foods.

A Sweet Treat: Butternut Squash Crumble with Vanilla Ice Cream

TOTAL TIME: 55 minutes PREP: 10 minutes COOK: 45 minutes SERVES: 6 to 8

When it comes to mixed textures, crumbles, crisps, and cobblers are desserts that kids seem to love almost instantly. Whether it's the ice cream on top or the crunch of the topping—I don't think I really will ever know why it's such a hit. I just know that even my pickiest eaters love making it as much as they love gobbling it up!

FILLING

8 ounces (225 g) packaged fresh butternut squash cubes or ½ butternut squash, peeled, seeded, and cubed
¼ cup (40 g) dried tart cherries
¼ cup (30 g) chopped walnuts or pecans
1½ teaspoons melted unsalted butter
1 teaspoon pure maple syrup
½ teaspoon ground cinnamon

TOPPING

½ cup (45 g) old-fashioned oats (gluten-free if needed)
¼ cup (30 g) all-purpose flour (gluten-free if needed)
¼ cup (50 g) sugar
⅓ teaspoon ground cinnamon
¼ cup (60 g) unsalted butter, melted
Vanilla ice cream for topping

① Preheat the oven to 350° (175°C).

② To make the filling, combine all the filling ingredients in a large pie pan or an 8 × 8-inch (20 × 20 cm) baking dish, stirring until everything is well coated, then spread the mixture evenly across the bottom of the pan.

③ To make the topping, stir together the oats, flour, sugar, and cinnamon in a large bowl. Drizzle the melted butter (be sure it's not hot) over the mixture and then squish it gently with clean hands until it's crumbly yet holds a shape.

④ Scatter the topping over the filling, completely covering it. It's OK to have a bit left over; in fact, you don't want too much on top or the crumble won't cook evenly.

⑤ Bake for 45 minutes, or until the topping is lightly browned.

⑥ Serve warm, topped with vanilla ice cream.

All Kids Can . . .

- Combine all the ingredients for the filling
- Stir the dry ingredients together and add the butter
- Squish the mixture with hands or a spoon
- Scatter the mixture over the filling
- Scoop ice cream onto each serving

PARENTING IN THE KITCHEN

Babies are programmed to explore the world with their hands and mouths. These two parts of our bodies work closely together to help our brains interpret information about things such as size, shape, temperature, and taste. But as kids get older, we often discourage getting messy—and that's a mistake. When kids experience the texture of the crumbly topping by feeling it first with their fingers and hands, they are more likely to put it in their mouths later.

PARSNIPS

Parents are often surprised at how easily kids take to parsnips! Closely related to carrots, parsnips become sweeter the longer they stay in the ground. In fact, some farmers use a process known as overwintering to increase the sweetness. The parsnips are kept in the ground over the entire winter and harvested in early spring. Choose small to medium sizes for optimal flavor. As with beets, if you buy parsnips with greens attached, you can sauté the greens using the recipe on page 20. And did you know? The potassium and folate in parsnips help keep our heart beating at just the right blood pressure, even in the face of danger!

EXPOSE
Hidden Treasures

In this turn-taking game, pearly white parsnip ribbons need to be lifted carefully, one by one, to find the treasure hiding beneath the pile. It's all part of the fun to get ready for the "Expand" section, when we'll be making a parsnip ribbon salad.

What you'll need:

- 3 medium-sized parsnips
- Vegetable peeler
- Safety gloves

- Small plastic animal that stands on four legs—which could be a zoo animal, a farm animal, or even a unicorn

What to do:

1 **KIDS:** Wash any dirt from the parsnips under running water. Chop off the ends and discard. Remove the outer layer of the parsnips with a vegetable peeler, wearing safety gloves, and discard those peels. Peel again, making as many ribbons as possible.

2 **PARENTS:** Hide the plastic animal beneath a pile of parsnip ribbons. (If you're doing this treasure hunt with younger kids, be careful not to intertwine the ribbons around the plastic critter. Simply pile them loosely on top.) The object of the game will be to uncover the animal without letting it fall over. The first one to uncover it wins!

3 **KIDS:** Taking turns with your parent, pull away one ribbon at a time, being careful not to let the animal fall over.

4 **PARENTS:** When the game is over, rinse the ribbons, pat them dry, and store them in a covered container in the fridge to use later in recipes. Or eat them now—that's even better!

How your child benefits

Turn taking not only teaches sportsmanship but is also a strong component of language development. In fact, that reciprocity of back-and-forth communication is one of the best skills to practice at the mealtime table for building social aptitude. Practicing fine motor skills also comes into play with the ribbon game. Using the pincer grasp (thumb and forefinger grasp) to carefully find the animal requires dexterity and control. Plus, if your child isn't keen on picking up new foods, it sets him up for success, because most kids will touch a new food if you're only asking them to do it with the tip of their thumb and the tip of their "pointer" finger. (Grasping a new food with the entire palm can be upsetting for kids who are sensitive to new textures.)

Parsnip-Carrot Mac 'n' Cheese

TOTAL TIME: 30 to 40 minutes PREP: 10 minutes COOK: 20 to 30 minutes SERVES: 6 to 8

When pureed parsnips and carrots are added to a roux and then made cheesy with Gruyère, the result is a pasta topping that's just the right color and rich flavor to rival any boxed macaroni and cheese—and won't you feel better serving this version instead? A roux (pronounced "roo") is the result of cooking flour and a fat together over heat and is used to thicken a sauce. As the liquid heats, its molecules begin to move around very rapidly. In addition, you'll be whisking to speed things up even more: You're making the molecules slam into the grains of starch in the flour. When that happens, the starch begins to absorb water. Now the mixture begins to thicken and presto: You've created a roux!

2 large carrots, peeled and cut into ¼-inch (6 mm) slices

2 medium parsnips, peeled and cut into ½-inch (13 mm) cubes

12 to 16 ounces (340 to 455 g) pasta, preferably elbows or penne (gluten-free if needed)

½ teaspoon chopped garlic (chopped garlic in a jar is easiest!)

3 tablespoons olive oil

3 tablespoons unsalted butter

1½ teaspoons all-purpose flour (gluten-free if needed)

½ cup (120 ml) chicken or vegetable broth

½ cup (120 ml) 2 percent milk

¾ cup (about 80 g) grated Gruyère

Salt and black pepper to taste

❶ Bring a medium pot of lightly salted water to a boil. Add the carrots and parsnips and simmer until tender. Drain.

❷ Bring a large pot of lightly salted water to a boil for the pasta. Cook per the package directions while preparing the cheese sauce.

❸ To make the cheese sauce, combine the cooked veggies and the garlic in a high-powered blender (such as a Blendtec), add 1 tablespoon of the olive oil, and puree.

❹ In a medium or large saucepan, combine the butter and the remaining 2 tablespoons olive oil. Once the butter begins to foam, begin to make a roux: Whisk the flour into the butter and cook for 1 minute. Tilt the pan slightly on the burner as you whisk to catch more of the liquid with each stroke. Put the pan flat on the burner again and add the broth and milk. Lightly whisk until the mixture begins to thicken.

5 Fold the vegetable puree into the roux with a wooden spoon. Add the grated cheese with a wooden spoon until combined. Season with salt and pepper. Remove from the heat and cover to keep warm if the pasta isn't ready.

6 Mix the pasta and "just enough" cheese sauce together before serving. (The shape and size of the pasta will determine how much sauce is needed, so add sauce gradually and reserve some to add to leftovers. Pasta will often absorb some of the sauce when leftovers are refrigerated. It's nice to have a bit more sauce to add the second day.) Add salt and pepper as necessary once more.

All Kids Can . . .

- Wash and dry the veggies
- Add ingredients to the blender
- Add salt and pepper to taste

Plus, Big Kids Can . . .

- Peel and slice the veggies (with adult supervision)
- Add pasta to the water to cook (with adult supervision)
- Make the roux (with adult supervision)
- Stir the cheese into the roux

PARENTING IN THE KITCHEN

Is it ever OK to sneak veggies into other foods? On the one hand, we always want to build trust with a hesitant eater, and that's why cooking together is so valuable. It makes the kids part of the process and gives them ownership in each dish. But, on the other hand, if it makes you feel better to add some veggie puree to a recipe on occasion, don't stress. Think about it: Every time you enjoy a freshly baked brownie with your child, it's not like you announce, "I knew you would like these! I put corn oil in them!" If you decide to "sneak" a little extra vegetable in a preferred food, be sure to eat it with your child. Then you can look for an opportunity to casually mention the hidden ingredient: "You know, I wasn't sure if I would like this new recipe. It has [fill in vegetable here] in it. But I do like it! It's yummy."

Parsnip Chips with a Kick

TOTAL TIME: 35 to 40 minutes PREP: 20 minutes COOK: 15 to 20 minutes SERVES: 4

These simple, crunchy chips have just a little kick with each bite, thanks to the combo of smoked paprika and Greek seasoning. (You'll find both of those in the spice aisle of your local supermarket.) For a creative variation, slice the parsnips into long sheets and use FunBites food cutters to cut out hearts, triangles, and other shapes to bake.

2 medium parsnips, washed, peeled, and sliced into very thin rounds (see Tip)
2 tablespoons avocado oil or olive oil
½ teaspoon Greek seasoning
½ teaspoon smoked paprika
Dash of salt

1 Preheat the oven to 425°F (215°C).

2 Toss the parsnip slices with the oil on a baking sheet (lined with foil for easy cleanup). Sprinkle the spices evenly on top and toss again to coat. Spread the slices evenly on the baking sheet, leaving space between each slice for even browning.

3 Roast for 10 minutes, then turn each slice over with tongs. Roast for 5 to 10 minutes more, depending on the thickness and size of the circles. Once they're lightly browned, turn the oven to broil to get a little extra crisp on the edges. Broil for up to 1 minute.

All Kids Can . . .

- Wash and dry the parsnips
- Toss the parsnip slices in the oil and seasonings
- Arrange the slices on the baking sheet

Plus, Big Kids Can . . .

- Use tongs to turn over each parsnip slice (with adult supervision)

PARENTING IN THE KITCHEN

Don't be afraid of introducing spices to your kids at an early age—in fact, the earlier the better. Research shows that babies still in the womb taste different flavors in the amniotic fluid. If moms are eating flavorful food, baby has already acquired a taste for strong flavors by the time she is born. Moreover, some hesitant eaters do better with foods that have a little spice to them—that extra kick may be just what they need to find certain foods appealing.

⪼ TIP ⪻

Use a section of the parsnip that's uniform in width so that all the circles are relatively the same diameter, to ensure that they cook evenly. Separate the smaller circles and cook those on a separate pan so that they can be removed from the oven sooner. When using FunBites, separate larger shapes from smaller shapes to ensure uniform cooking.

Rainbow Ribbon Salad

TOTAL TIME: 15 minutes **PREP:** 15 minutes **SERVES:** 4 to 6

....

If your child isn't fond of carrots yet, or you haven't explored them with the spring vegetables in chapter 2, it's fine to leave them out of this recipe. But carrots are typically one of the first vegetables kids learn to enjoy, because they are the sweetest. Just double the amount of parsnips if you leave out the carrots, but consider having the kids peel carrot ribbons to expose them to the fun colors and sweet aroma. You can also use the ribbons from the hidden treasure game from the "Expose" section on page 38.

2 medium parsnips
1 orange carrot
1 purple carrot
2 tablespoons extra virgin olive oil
1 tablespoon orange juice
1 tablespoon rice vinegar
Salt and black pepper to taste
¼ cup (40 g) raisins

....

1 Wash the parsnips and carrots. Chop off the ends and discard. Remove the outer layer with a vegetable peeler, wearing safety gloves, and discard those peels. Peel again, making as many ribbons as possible.

2 Whisk the oil, orange juice, and vinegar together to make a dressing. Add salt and pepper.

3 In a large bowl, toss together the parsnip and carrot ribbons and the raisins. Drizzle half of the dressing on top and toss again, coating very lightly. Add a touch more dressing if needed for taste, but the secret to this salad is keeping the ribbons light and airy on the plate; too much dressing can weigh them down.

All Kids Can . . .

- Wash and dry the veggies
- Whisk the dressing
- Toss the salad with the dressing
- Add salt and pepper to taste
- Peel the veggies (with adult supervision)

A Sweet Treat: Pears and Parsnips in Puff Pastry

TOTAL TIME: 50 minutes **PREP:** 20 minutes **COOK:** 30 minutes **SERVES:** 8

Say that five times fast! Get creative as you construct your pastry, topping it with stars or the shape of your choice. Puff pastry dough is made up of many thin layers stacked on top of each other, with globs of fat in between. As the dough heats up in the oven, spaces form between each layer as the fat melts, while the steam from the filling rises, pushing the light fluffy layers upward into puffed perfection.

¾ cup (180 ml) apple juice (See Parenting in the Kitchen)

1 parsnip, washed, peeled, and cut into ¾-inch (2 cm) pieces, about 1 cup (130 g)

3 tablespoons sugar, plus a couple pinches for topping

½ teaspoon ground cinnamon, plus a couple pinches for topping

1 large pear, cut into ¾-inch (2 cm) pieces, about 1 cup (130 g)

¼ cup (35 g) dried tart cherries (optional)

All-purpose flour (gluten-free if needed), for assembling the pastry

2 puff pastry sheets, thawed but still cold to the touch (see Tip)

1 egg

❶ Preheat the oven to 375°F (190°C).

❷ Heat the apple juice in a medium saucepan over low heat and simmer the chopped parsnip in the juice until just starting to become tender. Drain.

❸ Combine the sugar and cinnamon in a medium bowl. Add the chopped pear, parsnip, and cherries (if using) and toss them until they're evenly coated with the cinnamon sugar.

❹ Sprinkle flour on a clean counter or large cutting board. Unfold one pastry sheet, with the short side facing you. Using a cookie cutter in a simple shape easy for kids to handle (I love stars or diamonds), cut out three to six shapes from top to bottom along the left-hand third (lengthwise) of the pastry. Space the cutouts so that there will be enough dough (despite the holes) to fold the dough over onto the middle third, like closing the cover of a book. (The cut-out dough will be used to decorate the assembled pastry.)

5 Spoon half of the parsnip and pear mixture carefully onto the center section of the pastry—that is, top to bottom along the middle third—spreading evenly with all pieces flat on the dough.

6 Fold the left (holey) side over the mixture. Fold the right (solid) side over the center section. Pinch all the edges so that no filling will escape.

7 With a wide spatula, lift the filled pastry, carefully flipping it seam side down so that no filling bursts out during baking, onto a baking sheet lined with parchment paper. Beat the egg in a small bowl with a fork and brush the top of the pastry with the egg wash. Decorate by adding the cutouts to the top of the pastry and brush with egg wash. Sprinkle a pinch of cinnamon across the top for color and a pinch of sugar across the top for added sparkle. Take a sharp knife and make three small slits parallel to the short sides of the pastry, at the very top of the dough

(one toward the left, one in the center, and one toward the right) to allow steam to escape and to help the dough puff up.

8 Repeat steps 4 to 7 with the second pastry sheet and remaining filling.

9 Bake for 30 minutes, or until the pastry is puffy and golden brown. Rotate the pastry halfway through the baking if it appears to be browning too much on one side. Cool on a wire rack. Cut into equal servings, about eight pieces total.

All Kids Can . . .

- Wash and dry the pear and parsnip
- Cut the pear and parsnip with a kid-safe knife
- Help cut out shapes from the dough
- Help fold and pinch the edges of the dough
- Line the baking sheet with parchment paper
- Beat the egg with a fork
- Brush the pastry with the egg wash
- Sprinkle cinnamon and sugar on top of the pastry

Plus, Big Kids Can . . .

- Peel the parsnip (with adult supervision)
- Use a spatula to transfer the filled pastry to the baking sheet
- Cut slits into the pastry

PARENTING IN THE KITCHEN

The only reason I buy apple juice (in serving-size boxes of 6 ounces/177 ml) is to have small amounts in my pantry for recipes like this. Parsnips take on a flavor that mimics pears when simmered in apple juice, making pears and parsnips the perfect combination, while adding minimal sugar to this sweet treat. But when it comes to juice, in general consider limiting the amount your kids drink so it is no more than an occasional treat. Juice is nothing more than empty calories that cause a quick rise in blood sugar—which hinders appetite for healthier foods. Drinking juice can also contribute to tooth decay.[1]

TIP

Keep pastry sheets covered if you're not filling them right away to prevent drying out. Puff pastry sheets can be found in the frozen section of the supermarket and are typically 9 × 30 inches (23 × 76 cm) when unfolded and 3 × 10 inches (7.5 × 25 cm) when folded for this recipe. Bob's Red Mill's website describes how to make gluten-free puff pastry from scratch, if needed: bobsredmill.com/blog/recipes/step-by-step-gluten-free-puff-pastry.

SWEET POTATOES

You say "poe-tay-toe," I say "poe-tah-toe." It doesn't matter, because what we can both agree on is the word "sweet"! This orange, white, yellow, or purple tuberous root veggie could be a dessert—it's naturally that sugary and satisfying. Sweet potatoes balance our blood sugar, keep us regular, and contain antioxidants. Adding a bit of fat to a sweet potato recipe increases the absorption of beta-carotene, which is then converted into vitamin A. Be sure to try the purple variety for an extra boost of antioxidants!

EXPOSE

Dinosaurs and Volcanoes

Kids ages two to six love to pretend and use their hands as they tell a story. You'll see this happening when children play with dollhouses, superhero action figures, or miniature animals. Children approach fantasy play in a unique manner, and you'll learn more about your child's personality by observing how they set up a story in their minds. Here, dinosaurs can stomp across a landscape of mashed-potato volcanoes, or use the plastic animals from other activities in this book. Add different colors of potatoes and watch their imaginations run wild! Perhaps your child likes unicorns and decides on their own that the unicorns are playing in orange and white clouds. Let your child decide what the potatoes represent, how to manipulate the mashed veggies, and what role they will play in the cast of characters.

What you'll need:

- 3 (or more if lots of kids are joining in!) cooked whole russet-type baking potatoes, cooled
- 3 or more cooked whole sweet potatoes, cooled (see Tip on page 53 on slow-cooking them)
- Potato masher
- Baking sheet or large tray
- Plastic dinosaurs
- Bowl of water or damp washcloth (for cleaning messy fingers)
- Child-safe knife (plastic will do)

What to do:

1 KIDS: Cut open the potatoes and scoop out the inside to separate the flesh from the skins, which you can also use during pretend play. Use the potato masher to mash the flesh of the potatoes and place mounds of it on the baking sheet. The inside of the white potato might be the volcano, and the orange flesh of the sweet potato could be the lava flowing down the sides of the volcano, but it's up to you and your child to decide.

2 PARENTS: Encourage pretend play, helping your child hide the dinosaurs under the mashed potatoes, perhaps leaving some of the toy peeking out if the child is hesitant to dig in, so it's easier to grab. March the animals through the mash or make potato beds for them to take a rest and use the skins for blankets. Keep the bowl of water or a damp washcloth nearby if the mess is just too much for little fingers or to rinse off dinosaurs as needed. Most of all, have fun!

How your child benefits

Kids quickly fall in love with this messy game, getting braver with each attempt to dig into the potato mash. Bravery builds confidence, and in the long term it's the foundation for trying new and sometimes harder activities, including academic and physical challenges. Don't intervene if your child demonstrates her bravery while she makes the following recipes with you—she may very well pick up pieces of sweet potato and do a bit of squishing with her fingers to explore the texture again. She's learned through experience that her hands will predict what she's about to feel in her mouth. Pretend play—considered essential "symbolic play" by child development experts—is a safe way for kids to practice bravery, and it's a foundation for healthy social, emotional, and cognitive development in young children.

Sweet Potato Toast

TOTAL TIME: 10 minutes PREP: 6 minutes COOK: 4 minutes
MAKES: 4 to 6 pieces of toast

Did you know that you can cook slices of sweet potatoes just like toast in a pop-up toaster? Set out a variety of toppings for schmearing on top, or just enjoy the natural sweetness that only this vegetable can bring when it's warm with a slight crisp on the edges.

TIP

Slicing and then toasting in a pop-up toaster or toaster oven keeps the flesh of the sweet potato consistent with each bite, which can make a difference for a hesitant eater. (Kids who are "learning eaters" are learning about taste, texture, flavor, aroma, and many other aspects all in one bite. Sometimes, keeping one aspect consistent, like texture, helps them manage the other characteristics of a new food.)

One large sweet potato, washed and dried (but not peeled)

SCHMEARS AND TOPPINGS, OPTIONAL

Avocado, mashed and flavored with sea salt

Nut butters with banana slices on top

Sunflower seed butter with mini chocolate chips or pomegranate seeds on top

Mozzarella, tomatoes, and basil

Applesauce and ground cinnamon

Cut the sweet potato lengthwise into $\frac{1}{4}$-inch (6 mm) slices; a large potato will yield 4 to 6 slices. Toast on high, watching carefully that the slices don't burn. You may need to toast them more than once to reach your desired doneness. Schmear with your preferred toppings.

All Kids Can . . .

- Wash and dry the sweet potato
- Prepare and set out a few schmears and toppings

Plus, Big Kids Can . . .

- Slice the sweet potatoes (with adult supervision)

Sweet Potato Pancakes

TOTAL TIME: 25 to 30 minutes (not including sweet potato cooking time) **PREP:** 5 minutes
COOK: 20 minutes if using a large griddle **MAKES:** 12 pancakes

What's not to love about this delicious alternative to standard grain-based pancakes? Sweet potato pancakes offer an extra boost of vitamins A and B6, fiber, and antioxidants, plus they're made without flour. Providing round or star-shaped cookie cutters lets kids have fun at the table turning these veggie-based pancakes into an edible solar system. Or try FunBites food cutters to create all sorts of geometric shapes or kid-safe knives to let your child cut their own.

3 large eggs, beaten, plus 1 more if needed
1 cup (330 g) cooked and pureed sweet potato (see Tip)
½ teaspoon ground cinnamon
⅛ teaspoon ground nutmeg
Butter or oil for the pan
Pure maple syrup (optional)

1 In a large bowl, combine 3 eggs, the sweet potato puree, and the spices, mixing well. The batter should be the consistency of thick applesauce.

2 Heat a large griddle over medium heat and add enough butter or oil to keep the pancake batter from sticking. Test one pancake on the griddle to ensure that the batter is the right consistency. Add another beaten egg to thin the batter if needed.

3 Carefully spoon the batter to make pancakes that are no bigger than a baseball in diameter (about 2.5 inches/6.5 cm), so that they will be easier to flip, but make sure they're big enough to use with the cookie cutters. Brown one side, flip, and brown the other; this should take about 5 minutes per side. (Note: You won't see bubbles appear in this batter, as you would in traditional pancakes.) Repeat until all the batter is used, adding more butter to the griddle as needed.

④ Cut with cookie cutters or cut into various phases of the moon! Rather than pouring syrup on these pancakes, have kids drizzle it in thin circles around one circular shape just for dipping—call those the rings of Saturn. (Dipping into syrup means less syrup—and less sugar—at breakfast.)

All Kids Can . . .

- Mix the pancake ingredients
- Use cookie cutters to create planets, moons, stars, and so on
- Drizzle the syrup to create rings of Saturn

Plus, Big Kids Can . . .

- Pour batter onto the hot griddle and flip the pancakes

BYO (Build Your Own) Sweet Potatoes

TOTAL TIME: 15 minutes (not including sweet potato baking time) **PREP:** 15 minutes
SERVES: 6 with leftover sweet potato puree

Put the kids in charge of setting up a construction station to build your own baked sweet potatoes! Assembling a variety of toppings is quick and easy. Kids may not taste all the toppings, but chopping up the roasted veggies or crumbling the cheese continues to expose them to a variety of foods. Many of the toppings, like chopped nuts or cheese, can be kept in small jars in the pantry or refrigerator. Just screw off the lid and add a spoon to each jar when assembling any kind of "build your own" bar. Puree the potato to fill the skins with a pastry bag for a fancy touch!

6 baked sweet potatoes (see Tip)

TOPPINGS

Blue cheese crumbles
Chopped chives
Chopped nuts
Chopped roasted vegetables, such as broccoli, cauliflower, and parsnips (mixed or in separate dishes)
Dried fruits, such as chopped dates or cranberries
Feta cheese crumbles
Grated mozzarella
Ground nutmeg, cinnamon, or sea salt (in shakers)
Hamburger crumbles (cooked)
Melted unsalted butter
Melted coconut oil
Mini marshmallows
Roasted coconut chips or toasted unsweetened coconut
Sour cream or plain 2 percent Greek yogurt

1 Carefully cut one long slit from end to end in each sweet potato, cutting them into two halves or keeping the halves attached, like an open book. If you're feeling fancy, gently scoop out the inside of the sweet potatoes and mash it, save the skins, and use the mashed potato to fill a pastry bag. Using various tips, fill each skin again with the sweet potato mash, creating designs on top. Otherwise just leave the inside of the potatoes intact. Place the baked potatoes on small microwavable plates.

2 Set up a construction station of favorite toppings, using ramekins or small bowls.

3 Invite everyone to warm their potato in the microwave, if needed, and fill with favorite toppings.

All Kids Can . . .

- Cut the sweet potatoes open with a kid-safe knife
- Scoop out the insides of the potatoes
- Help fill pastry bags (if using)
- Refill the potato skins
- Push the buttons on the microwave (with adult supervision) to reheat the potatoes

- Chop toppings (where necessary) with a kid-safe knife
- Arrange toppings in serving bowls

 TIP

To bake the potatoes evenly, preheat the oven to 400°F (200°C), wash the potatoes well, and pierce the skin three to five times with a fork. Lightly oil the skins and wrap each loosely in foil so that steam can escape from either end. Bake until tender, 45 to 60 minutes. Carefully remove them from the oven and unwrap. You can also cook them in a slow cooker (see Tip on page 53).

PARENTING IN THE KITCHEN

Notice which toppings your kids prefer, and whether or not they like them in combinations. Ask, "What is it about those toppings that make them some of your favorites?" Encourage kids to use words that describe the foods instead of responding "I just like them." Model words like "crunchy," "savory," or "meltable" to help kids pinpoint why a food feels or tastes good in their mouth. Then, when trying another new food, you can use those terms to bridge the gap. "This feta cheese is crumbly like the sausage you liked, and a bit salty, too."

A Sweet Treat: Sweet Potato Beary Bar Cookies

TOTAL TIME: 50 minutes (not including sweet potato cooking time) **PREP:** 20 minutes
COOK: 7 minutes for the crust, 20 to 25 minutes for the filling **MAKES:** 12 cookies

These delectable bar cookies have a little extra fun baked right into the crust! Kids love to help crush the little teddy bear–shaped cookies that are the foundation for the bar cookie. Press one whole bear into the cookie crust so that when your kids bite into the bar, they'll find a bear hiding at the bottom—fast asleep, having sweet potato dreams. For a delicious gluten-free option, use 20 ounces (566 g) Annie's Gluten-Free Cocoa & Vanilla Bunny Cookies. Now you'll be hiding bunnies instead of bears!

CRUST

½ cup (120 ml) melted coconut oil, plus enough for coating the pan

One 10-ounce (283 g) box honey tiny bear cookies, such as Nabisco Teddy Grahams

One 10-ounce (283 g) box chocolate tiny bear cookies, such as Nabisco Teddy Grahams

COOKIE TOP

⅓ cup (60 g) lightly packed brown sugar

1 large egg, at room temperature

1 teaspoon pure vanilla extract

1½ cups (485 g) mashed sweet potatoes, at room temperature (see the slow cooker Tip on page 53)

1 cup (115 g) coconut flour (see Tip)

1 tablespoon ground cinnamon

1 teaspoon baking powder (gluten-free if needed)

¼ teaspoon salt

3 tablespoons melted coconut oil

1 Preheat the oven to 375°F (190°C).

2 To make the crust, prepare a brownie or muffin pan by coating the bottom and sides of each cup with warm (not hot) melted coconut oil.

❸ Set aside 6 honey bears and 6 chocolate bears before dumping both boxes of cookies into a food processor. Pulse until you have very coarse crumbs. (Alternative method: Dump the teddy bear cookies into a plastic bag and let the kids crush them using a rolling pin. The result won't be as consistent, but it's a lot more fun!)

❹ Transfer the crushed cookies to a large bowl and slowly mix in just enough coconut oil so that the crushed cookies hold together when you squeeze them. You may have some oil left over, depending on how coarsely you ground the crumbs.

❺ Place one teddy bear cookie in the center of each individual section of the pan, then press some of the crumb mixture around the bear, allowing just a thin coating over the bear. Aim for a crust no thicker than ¼ inch (6 mm).

❻ Bake for 7 minutes. Remove the pan from the oven and let cool. Do not remove the crusts from the pan.

❼ To make the cookie top, reduce the oven heat to 350°F (180°C). Combine the sugar, egg, and vanilla in a large bowl, mixing with a hand mixer or a wooden spoon until no lumps remain. Add the mashed sweet potatoes and mix until smooth.

8 In a medium bowl, mix the flour, cinnamon, baking powder, and salt. Slowly add the flour mixture to the sweet potato mixture, stirring until they are thoroughly combined. Drizzle the coconut oil over the resulting thick batter and mix well.

10 Spoon the mixture onto each crust, filling to ¼ inch (6 mm) from the top of the pan. Bake for 20 to 25 minutes, until a toothpick inserted into the center of a cookie comes out clean.

11 Remove the pan from the oven and allow the cookies to cool completely. Then use a knife to loosen the side of each bar before removing them from the pan.

All Kids Can . . .

- Prep the pan with melted coconut oil
- Send teddy bear cookies down the chute of the food processor or crush the cookies in a plastic bag
- Squish crushed cookies and warm coconut oil to make the crust
- Place a teddy bear cookie at the bottom of each section of the pan
- Press the crumb mixture into the pan
- Mix the topping and spoon it onto the crust.

TIP

Coconut flour is not only high in fiber, protein, and healthy fats, but it also gives baked goods a heavier texture that matches perfectly with the crust in this oh-so-satisfying dessert.

TURNIPS

I'm always surprised at how many kids prefer mashed turnips to mashed potatoes. The texture is only slightly different—a bit less starchy. Still, for picky eaters, texture is a big deal, and mashed potatoes have a heavy mouthfeel that learning eaters can find difficult to swallow. For adventurous eaters, the slight variation may be the perfect bridge to learning to love turnips, and for hesitant eaters, turnips may be the bridge to mashed potatoes. The indoles and fiber in turnips keep the cells in our body healthy and help us stay regular!

EXPOSE

Mr. Turnip Head

Put a goofy spin on an old favorite by creating silly turnip heads using parts from the Mr. Potato Head toy. Playskool makes creative versions of Mr. Potato Head featuring the latest movie action heroes, but the "old school" version is just as entertaining and can usually be bought for a buck or two at any thrift store. Medium-sized turnips are ideal for this activity. The turnips will need to be steamed for a few minutes (then cooled) to make the pieces easier to insert.

What you'll need:

- Fresh turnips—keep the greens attached for hair! (If you can't find turnips with greens, include a bunch of herbs or lettuce leaves and use the plastic hats that come with Mr. Potato Head to secure the green hair in place.)

- Pot with steamer insert and lid
- Mr. Potato Head parts—eyes, shoes, hats, and so on

What to do:

1 **KIDS:** Wash any dirt from the turnips under running water.

2 **PARENTS:** Steam the turnips just slightly (see Tip). Place them in a strainer and run them under cold water to cool completely. Small to medium turnips won't need to be peeled, but larger ones may have tough skin that needs to be pared away.

3 **KIDS:** Dry the cooled turnips with a kitchen towel.

4 **PARENTS AND KIDS:** Create silly turnip characters! Who can make one that looks like Daddy?

> TIP

To keep the greens from wilting while you're steaming the turnips, put the turnips in the pot with the greens on the outside, and use the lid to secure the entire arrangement. Be careful that the greens don't hang so low that they are charred on the stove's burner.

How your child benefits

When kids younger than four do this activity, they are practicing vocabulary skills when naming Mr. Turnip Head's body parts, along with developing skills that therapists call "visual-form constancy" and "understanding representational objects."[2] Basically, that means that very small children will recognize the piece that represents an eye and likewise recognize where the eye should go, even though it's a different shape, size, and color than their own eye.

Mashed Turnips with Bacon and Chives

TOTAL TIME: 20 minutes PREP: 20 minutes COOK: 10 minutes SERVES: 4

Keep your child's personality in mind when introducing a new food, and look for common ground. For this recipe, almost everyone loves the satisfaction of mashing! Pediatric therapists call this "heavy work," because it requires a child to push hard into the cooked vegetable, mushing and squishing to get to the desired consistency. Not only is mashing vegetables fun, but it also activates your child's sensory system, increasing awareness of his body and how it works.

1½ cups (360 ml) chicken or vegetable broth
3 pounds (1.4 kg) fresh turnips, peeled and cut into 1-inch (2.5 cm) cubes
3 strips applewood-smoked bacon (see Tip)
2 tablespoons unsalted butter
Pinch of garlic powder or ½ teaspoon minced roasted garlic (minced garlic from a jar is also fine!)
1 scallion, green parts only, finely chopped
Salt and black pepper to taste

1 Bring the broth to a boil in a large saucepan, add the turnip cubes, lower the heat, and cook until very tender, about 10 minutes.

2 While the turnips are cooking, fry the bacon in a skillet over medium heat until it's crispy, turning the strips so they brown evenly. Remove the bacon from the skillet and lay the strips out on paper towels to soak up the grease.

3 Drain the cooked turnips and mash them with a handheld potato masher while they're still warm, incorporating the butter and garlic as you work. The mash should be chunky.

4 Crumble the bacon and stir the bacon and scallion into the mash. Season with salt and pepper and serve.

All Kids Can . . .

- Wash and dry the turnips
- Pour the broth into the pot
- Chop the scallion with a kid-safe knife
- Mash the turnips
- Crumble the cooled bacon and scallion into the mash and stir
- Add salt and pepper to taste

Plus, Big Kids Can . . .

- Peel the turnips (with adult supervision)

- Cut the turnips into cubes (with adult supervision)
- Cook the bacon (with adult supervision)

TIP

As much as I love a scrumptious, crispy slice of bacon, the families I work with know that it is a "sometimes food." Add it in small amounts on occasion to include a savory component to a recipe. Choose bacon that is nitrate-free and lower in sodium than other brands. Center-cut bacon has less fat and can be slightly more expensive, but you don't need much for recipes in this book. Turkey bacon is lower in saturated fat and sometimes lower in sodium. Keep in mind it's a processed meat, so use sparingly. A little goes a long way!

Green Apple and Turnip Straw Salad

TOTAL TIME: 15 minutes SERVES: 4

Slivers of tart green apple and savory turnips are piled high like stacks of straw to eat piece by piece or scooped up with a "pitch" fork. Some kids are hesitant to try salads because they can be tricky to eat with utensils. Not so with these crunchy and tangy matchsticks! Each bite is loaded with potassium, fiber, and vitamin C.

2 Granny Smith apples (another tart variety such as Pink Lady would work as a substitute—or use one of each)
Juice of 1 lime
1 large turnip, about the size of the 2 apples together
¼ cup (35 g) roasted almonds, chopped (see Parenting in the Kitchen)

1 Wash the apples and slice them into skinny matchsticks, leaving the skin on. Immediately put the apple matchsticks in a medium bowl and toss them with some of the lime juice to stop any browning.

2 Wash and peel the turnip and slice it into matchsticks.

3 Toss the turnip and apple matchsticks together, adding more lime juice if needed for extra flavor. Add the almonds, toss, and serve.

All Kids Can . . .

- Wash and dry the apples and turnip
- Use a kid-safe knife to make apple and turnip matchsticks
- Juice the lime
- Toss the apples with the lime juice
- Add the almonds and toss again

Plus, Big Kids Can . . .

- Peel the turnips (with adult supervision)

The photo above demonstrates a young child using a "cat paw" to hold a slice of food steady while cutting with a child-safe knife. By bending the knuckles slightly, the fingertips are protected. When advancing to a sharp knife, teach your older child to curl the fingertips beneath the knuckles even more and to always cut straight down, never toward the stabilizing hand. If using a portable cutting board that might slip, place a damp paper towel underneath to prevent it from sliding on the counter.

PARENTING IN THE KITCHEN

As a feeding therapist, I usually advise parents to avoid giving whole nuts to kids until they are four years old, and many pediatricians agree. Why? With kids under age three, we worry about immature oral motor skills, but nuts are a choking risk even for slightly older kids, because preschool-age kids are so distractible. For young children, chop all nuts until they are the size of a pea.

Root Veggie Soup with Turnips and Carrots

TOTAL TIME: 35 to 40 minutes PREP: 15 minutes COOK: 20 to 25 minutes SERVES: 6 to 8

Nothing beats soothing, warm vegetable soup for lunch or dinner on a winter day—and the more veggies in the soup, the more nutrients it offers to growing bodies. Your child's winter soup adventure can begin with this chunky dish made from simple turnips and orange carrots. Soups like this one are best served in a shallow bowl with only a touch of broth over the vegetables. The turnips and carrots should be sticking up above the broth to make them more inviting. Set the table with a fork for snagging the vegetables and a straw for sipping up the broth, along with a spoon to eat both at once.

4 orange carrots (see Parenting in the Kitchen)
2 small turnips
2 tablespoons coconut oil
1 small onion, finely chopped
2 teaspoons chopped garlic
1 sprig fresh rosemary
2 sprigs fresh thyme
4 cups (960 ml) very hot chicken or vegetable broth
1 cup (240 ml) very hot water
Salt and black pepper to taste

1 Peel the carrots and turnips and chop them into bite-size cubes.

2 Melt the coconut oil in a large, heavy pot over medium-low heat. Add the onion and garlic and sauté until the onion becomes translucent. Add the carrots and turnips, stirring to coat them evenly with the coconut oil. Add the rosemary and thyme.

3 Turn the heat up to medium-high. Add the broth and water to the pot and simmer for 15 to 20 minutes, paying attention to make sure the vegetables soften just slightly and retain a slight crunch—don't let them get mushy. (Pierce with a fork to test.)

4 Remove and discard the sprigs of herbs. Season with salt and pepper and serve.

All Kids Can . . .

- Wash and dry the veggies
- Chop the veggies using a kid-safe knife
- Add the veggies and herbs to the pot
- Add salt and pepper to taste. Use a small spoon and blow on the soup gently before tasting to help it cool!

Plus, Big Kids Can . . .

- Peel the veggies (with adult supervision)
- Cut the onion with a sharp knife (with adult supervision), using a cat paw (see page 65)
- Cook the vegetables and add hot water and broth (with adult supervision)

PARENTING IN THE KITCHEN

Try cooking this soup with carrots in other colors—purple, red, yellow, and white. If you don't have access to a fresh source of these less-familiar varieties, you should be able to find them—labeled "rainbow carrots"—in the frozen foods section of the grocery store. For adventurous eaters, you can add a mix of new colors right off the bat. With hesitant veggie eaters, you might want to add one color at a time. (A small caveat: Don't cook the purple carrots in the broth itself. Steam and add them separately— or the soup will turn a muddy shade of purple. Although . . . if your child adores purple, definitely do that.) Add other root vegetables each time you make the soup. Remember to cook the vegetables so that they are tender but still a bit firm—you want the veggies to be easily identifiable in a child's mouth.

A Sweet Treat: Monogrammed Mini Turnip Pies

TOTAL TIME: 1 hour 10 minutes **PREP:** 25 minutes **COOK:** 45 minutes **SERVES:** 4 to 5

These adorable mini pies take on the taste and texture of another fall favorite, apple pie! The secret is simmering the turnips in apple juice first. Choose small to medium turnips for this recipe, because smaller turnips are sweeter. This recipe calls for making individual pies, baked in four or five 6-ounce (177 ml) ramekins—be sure to monogram a pie for each member of the family by cutting out letters from the dough and putting first and last initials on the top of individual pies. Finish off by getting the kids involved in the final prep by teaching them the science of making whipped cream.

3 medium apples
Lemon juice for the apples
3 small to medium turnips, no bigger than the apples
¾ cup (180 ml) apple juice, plus more if needed
2 tablespoons melted coconut oil
⅛ teaspoon light brown sugar
Pinch of cinnamon
¼ cup (40 g) dried cranberries
1 rolled pie crust, such as Pillsbury's, at room temperature and ready to roll out (for a gluten-free crust, try Glutino Perfect Pie Crust Mix, making it ahead of time and keeping the dough in the refrigerator)
Flour for rolling out the crust
1 tablespoon solid coconut oil
1 large egg, whisked

HOMEMADE WHIPPED CREAM

1 cup (240 ml) whipping cream, very cold
1½ tablespoons granulated sugar, optional
1 teaspoon ground cinnamon, optional
¼ teaspoon ground nutmeg, optional

1 Preheat the oven to 350°F (180°C).

2 Peel and core the apples and chop them into bite-size pieces, sprinkling with lemon juice to stop any browning. Peel the turnips and chop them into comparable pieces.

3 Bring the apple juice to a boil in a medium saucepan, then add the turnips, ensuring that the juice covers all

the pieces. Turn the heat down and gently simmer for 10 minutes. Drain.

④ Combine the melted coconut oil, brown sugar, and cinnamon in a large bowl. Add the apples, turnips, and cranberries, stirring to coat evenly.

⑤ Unroll the pie crust onto a floured countertop and lightly flour the top surface. Press an upside-down ramekin into the pie crust to cut out four or five circles (depending on the number of mini pies you want to make) along one side. With the remaining dough, kids can use a kid-safe knife to cut out the first and last initials of themselves and other family members, which will be added to the top of each pie crust as a monogram. Gently remove the remaining edges of pie crust (anything that's not a circle or letter) and discard, or let kids play with the extra pieces and perhaps bake them on a baking sheet.

⑥ Warm a dollop of the solid coconut oil between your fingertips and lightly coat the edges of each ramekin. Fill each ramekin almost to the top with the turnip mixture.

⑦ Using a spatula, lift each of the circle cutouts and place them on the surface of the mixture in the ramekins. The edges of the pie dough should just meet the edges of the ramekin. Brush the pie dough with some of the whisked egg. Lay the pie-dough initials on top, overlapping the letters slightly to form a monogram. Brush the initials with whisked egg.

⑧ Top each of the individual pies with a loose tent of aluminum foil, to prevent the crust from browning too quickly. Bake for 20 minutes.

⑨ Remove the foil tents. Continue baking for another 20 to 25 minutes, until the crusts on the pies are lightly browned.

⑩ Remove the pies from the oven and let them cool slightly, until the ramekins are safe to touch.

⑪ Meanwhile, make the Homemade Whipped Cream (see Kitchen Science). Place a metal bowl in the freezer for at least 5 minutes, then remove and pour in the whipping cream. Holding the bowl at a slight angle, use a whisk to whip the cream in little circular motions until soft peaks begin to form. If you're not going to include any other flavorings, keep whipping until stiff peaks form; otherwise, add the sugar, cinnamon, and nutmeg and continue to whip. You'll know you're there when the bowl is full of snowy white mountains that won't collapse when you stop whipping. A hand mixer means less work, but bigger kids enjoy doing it by hand! It only takes a few more minutes and gives better control over the final texture.

⑫ Top the pies with whipped cream and serve immediately.

All Kids Can . . .

- Wash and dry the apples and turnips
- Chop the apples and turnips with a kid-safe knife
- Combine the filling ingredients and stir to coat
- Roll out the pie crust
- Press the ramekin into the pie dough to make circles
- Make initials with a kid-safe knife
- Play with the extra dough!
- Coat the edges of the ramekins with coconut oil
- Fill the ramekins with the turnip mixture
- Top the ramekins with the dough circles
- Brush the dough with whisked egg
- Add the monogram to the crust
- Add whipped cream when serving

Plus, Big Kids Can . . .

- Peel the apples and turnips (with adult supervision)
- Cook the turnips (with adult supervision)
- Whip the cream with a whisk

KITCHEN SCIENCE

Just how does that white liquid turn to the fluffy whipped solid known as whipped cream? I'm not sure exactly how many air bubbles it takes, but it must be millions that incorporate into the liquid as the whisk does its magic. As the cream begins to froth, the outer membranes of fat globules begin to break down and the fat seals in the air bubbles, creating stiffer and stiffer peaks. Don't whip too much or you'll have butter!

Part Two

SPRING VEGETABLES

Just as the daffodils begin to peek through the soil, talk to your kids about what they would like to plant in a family garden. It doesn't have to be a large bed in the backyard—even a few pots on the windowsill will do. How about growing some edibles instead of only decorative plants? Try a space saver like cucumber vines climbing up a trellis just outside your front door. Whatever type of garden you choose, your child will benefit from digging and planting in the soil. In fact, research shows that when kids are engaged in gardening activities they feel better, their mood improves, and they have less overall anxiety—which allows them to learn better, too! On top of that, I guarantee that foods they grow are foods they're more likely to pop into their mouths.

ASPARAGUS

Asparagus contains the mighty antioxidant known as vitamin K, which helps prevent inflammation. Short, thick spears of asparagus have more sweet flesh (ideal for purees), while long, skinny stalks have very little flesh and provide a lovely outer crunch when roasted. Which is better is always a big debate among foodies, but it comes down to preference, so try both! Always snap off the woody ends, no matter the thickness of the spear, to ensure that it won't be tough or stringy for kids. While holding most of the spear in one fist, hold the end (without the flower-like head) between your thumb and forefinger and bend until it breaks. Note: The terms *stalk* and *spear* are used interchangeably throughout this chapter and are not dependent on the thickness of the asparagus.

EXPOSE

Asparagus Log Cabins

This is your house and you are the architect! You'll find two different options for the mortar in this activity, a cream cheese version and a meringue. The powdered sugar and cream cheese bind together for an excellent cement-like mortar, but it's very sweet and not meant for kids to consume a lot of! Still, if they dip a piece of raw asparagus into a tiny bit of mortar and take a crunch, it's a sweet introduction to a new veggie that may lead to asparagus love in the upcoming recipes in this chapter.

What you'll need:

- 1 large bundle fresh asparagus, ideally of different widths and colors, per person
- Small empty milk, cream, or orange juice carton, per person
- Sharp scissors (for parents)
- Kid-safe knife for spreading the mortar and trimming asparagus

For the mortar, per person (see Tip for a meringue alternative):

- 3 tablespoons (45 g) cream cheese, at room temperature
- 1 tablespoon (15 g) unsalted butter, at room temperature
- ½ teaspoon pure vanilla extract
- 2 cups (240 g) confectioners' sugar

What to do:

❶ KIDS: Wash any dirt from the asparagus and snap off the woody ends at the bottom of the stalks. Who can snap the loudest?

❷ PARENTS: Wash out the milk containers and wipe down the sides, then let them dry. Using the point of the scissors, add a window or two to each box, if desired. Staple the top of the carton back into its roof-like shape.

❸ PARENTS AND KIDS: Using a hand mixer or a high-powered blender, blend the cream cheese, butter, and vanilla until smooth. Gradually add the sugar until a consistency for thick mortar is achieved.

4 KIDS: Spread the mortar on one wall of the milk carton house at a time and add asparagus "logs" horizontally or vertically. Continue until the sides and the roof are complete. Use a kid-safe knife to trim the asparagus to size, or simply bite off the end that you don't need. Hungry? Raw asparagus is a crunchy treat. Try it dipped in a bit of mortar—that's edible, too!

To make a traditional gingerbread house mortar, beat together 1½ tablespoons meringue powder (such as Wilton's, typically found at craft stores), 2 cups (240 g) confectioners' sugar, and 2½ tablespoons water until peaks form, 7 to 10 minutes on low with a heavy-duty mixer or 10 to 12 minutes on high with a handheld mixer; follow the package instructions for best results.

How your child benefits

Your child is hard at work, using spatial and math skills as she creates her own architectural masterpiece. She's also developing her sense of proprioception—the awareness of where her body is in space as she moves. Proprioception is the sensory information that enables her to push the asparagus into the mortar with just the right amount of pressure. That same feedback is used in our mouths, when we decide how hard we must press down with our teeth to break through raw vegetables or to gently nibble softer, steamed asparagus. As you and your child are building together, model biting into raw asparagus and talk about how hard you had to bite for the thicker stalks or how gently you used your front teeth to snip off a piece of a skinny stalk. If your child is a picky eater but she's willing to bite into asparagus and spit out the remnant, that's terrific! If she's biting, chewing, and swallowing as she builds, that's wonderful, too. Always celebrate each tiny step and focus on the fun.

Roasted Asparagus with Sweet Mandarin Oranges

TOTAL TIME: 25 minutes PREP: 10 minutes COOK: 12 minutes SERVES: 4

Fresh mandarins, peeled and ready to burst with each bite, give this dish a familiar citrusy note that kids love! It's my go-to recipe whenever I need a side dish for community get-togethers because it's so quick and appealing to kids of all ages.

1½ pounds (680 g) asparagus
1 tablespoon olive oil
Salt and black pepper to taste
2 large mandarin oranges (zested for topping if you like)

VINAIGRETTE

2 large mandarin oranges, zested and juiced (this will yield about ½ cup/120 ml juice and 1 tablespoon zest)
2 tablespoons honey
2 tablespoons sherry vinegar
½ cup (120 ml) extra virgin olive oil
Salt and black pepper to taste

1 Preheat the oven to 400°F (200°C).

2 Wash and dry the asparagus, then snap off the woody ends and discard them. Toss the asparagus with the olive oil, salt, and pepper and arrange the stalks on a baking sheet.

3 Roast the asparagus until it's slightly tender, about 12 minutes for stalks of medium thickness.

4 While the asparagus is roasting, make the Vinaigrette (see Tip): Whisk together the orange zest, juice, honey, and vinegar. Slowly whisk in the olive oil to create an emulsion.

⑤ Peel the remaining 2 mandarin oranges and separate the segments, removing any obvious strings. Toss the orange segments with the roasted asparagus on the baking sheet and return the sheet to the oven for 1 minute to warm the fruit.

⑥ Remove the baking sheet from the oven and drizzle half of the vinaigrette over the hot asparagus and orange segments. Add a bit more zest on top if you want to be fancy. Serve the asparagus warm with the remaining vinaigrette available on the table. (Some people like asparagus, but other people just like a little asparagus with their vinaigrette.)

All Kids Can . . .

- Wash and dry the asparagus, snapping off the woody ends
- Toss the asparagus with the oil and seasonings
- Arrange the asparagus on a baking sheet
- Whisk the ingredients for the vinaigrette
- Peel the mandarin oranges, separate the segments, and remove the strings
- Add the oranges to the pan (with adult supervision)

When making any vinaigrette, taste and adjust for your palate! Some people prefer more acid (like orange juice) in a dressing, but others like more sweetness or more fat. That's the beauty of tasting—it helps us find out what we like and what we don't. Teach your child to never be afraid of a yuck, because you can often find a way to turn it into a yum!

KITCHEN SCIENCE

Why does asparagus make our pee smell funny? Blame it on a sulfurous compound that also makes us turn up our noses at rotten eggs. Fortunately, we can't detect the sulfur when we eat asparagus, but when our digestive system breaks down the food, it creates an unusual smell that many people can't help but notice when they pee! Although a majority of people have the nose to detect this odor, up to 40 percent are oblivious to the smell. It's possible that this awareness (or lack thereof) is genetically based.

Crispy Asparagus Bundles

TOTAL TIME: 20 minutes PREP: 10 minutes COOK: 10 minutes SERVES: 4 to 6

Everything tastes better with crispy prosciutto! These make a terrific appetizer. Encourage kids to chop up any leftovers to add to a salad the next day. It's a surprising element that takes the basic dinner salad up a notch . . . that is, if you have leftovers. These little bundles disappear in a jiffy!

1 pound (455 g) thin asparagus spears
1 tablespoon extra virgin olive oil
Salt and black pepper to taste
6 or 7 prosciutto slices

1 Position an oven rack about 6 inches (15 cm) below the heating element and set the oven on broil to preheat.

2 Wash and dry the asparagus, then snap off the woody ends and discard them. Toss the asparagus lightly with the olive oil, salt, and pepper.

3 Gather three spears of asparagus and wrap them in a slice of prosciutto: Start at one end of the slice and wrap carefully around the spears, allowing a bit of overlap with each wrap. Place the bundles on a baking sheet, leaving space between them to allow the prosciutto to crisp.

4 Broil for about 5 minutes, then remove the baking sheet from the oven and turn each bundle over with tongs, being careful that they don't unwrap in the process. Return the sheet to the broiler and continue to cook for about 5 minutes more, until the prosciutto is crispy. The timing will vary according to the size of the bundle.

⑤ Allow the bundles to cool slightly before serving, and eat them with fingers.

All Kids Can . . .

- Wash and dry the asparagus, snapping off the woody ends
- Toss the asparagus with oil and seasonings
- Wrap the asparagus spears with prosciutto

- Arrange the asparagus bundles on the baking sheet

TIP

Broiling requires close supervision of the food and the child, so that neither gets burned! Crack the oven door just slightly once you suspect the food is beginning to brown, and be ready with your oven mitt to remove the baking sheet. Younger kids might need to observe from a distance.

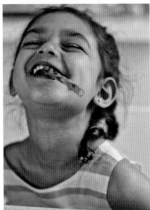

Crunchy Asparagus Explosion

TOTAL TIME: 35 minutes PREP: 15 minutes COOK: 20 minutes SERVES: 4

Got a kid who loves the flavor combo of sweet and tangy? Add a little crunch and you've got this explosive salad recipe, which brings together strawberries, asparagus, and nuts, all topped with a zingy dressing! The dressing can be prepared ahead of time, or you can do the roasting and blending at the same time you're prepping the asparagus.

ROASTED STRAWBERRY DRESSING

1 cup (140 g) strawberries, washed, hulled, and halved
¼ cup (60 ml) balsamic vinegar
2 tablespoons extra virgin olive oil
1 tablespoon honey
1 tablespoon finely chopped shallot
1 teaspoon Dijon mustard
½ teaspoon dried thyme (optional)
Salt and black pepper to taste

SALAD

12 ounces (340 g) asparagus, preferably thin spears
½ cup (55 g) almond slivers (see Parenting in the Kitchen)
1 pound (455 g) strawberries, washed, hulled, and sliced
¼ cup (25 g) crumbled goat or blue cheese (optional)

❶ To make the Roasted Strawberry Dressing, preheat the oven to 425°F (215°C). Spread the halved strawberries evenly on a rimmed baking sheet lined with parchment. Roast for 15 to 20 minutes, until caramelized. (For more about caramelization, see page 195.) The color of the strawberries will deepen and you may see some browning around the edges. A bit of syrup will be visible on the baking sheet.

❷ Put all the dressing ingredients, including the roasted strawberries, into a blender and blend until smooth.

3 Meanwhile, to make the salad, bring a medium pot of water to a boil. Wash and snap off the woody ends of the asparagus. Slice the asparagus stalks at an angle into 1-inch (2.5 cm) pieces and blanch them (see Tip).

4 Toast the almonds in a pan over medium heat for 1 to 2 minutes, until they're golden brown. (This step adds a depth of flavor and softens the almonds just a bit.)

5 Toss the asparagus and the sliced strawberries with just enough dressing to coat lightly. Add the cheese (if using). Reserve any remaining dressing for future use or include in a small ramekin on each plate for dipping.

All Kids Can . . .

- Wash and dry the strawberries
- Remove hulls from the strawberries
- Wash and dry the asparagus, snapping off the woody ends
- Place the dressing ingredients in a blender

- Turn the blender on and off (with adult supervision)
- Crumble the cheese (if using)

Plus, Big Kids Can . . .

- Toast the almonds (with adult supervision)

 TIP

Blanching brings out a bright color in vegetables, making greens more vivid and appealing. It also keeps veggies crunchy but adds a touch of water, making it easier to keep all the pieces together as we chew. Most kids prefer the crunch of a blanched vegetable over a raw one, even with a simple platter of crudités (typically raw veggies served with a dipping sauce). To blanch, carefully put pieces of veggies in boiling water for 1 to 3 minutes and remove immediately with a slotted spoon, transferring the vegetables to an ice bath (a large bowl of ice water) to stop the cooking. Cool, drain, and pat the veggies dry to enjoy the crisp crunch! Blanched veggies store well in a covered container in the refrigerator for up to a four days.

PARENTING IN THE KITCHEN

If you have more almond slivers on hand than you need for this recipe, toast the extra to have some available for kids' snacks or to garnish other recipes. Remember that even for kids ages two to four who have molars and demonstrate safe chewing for nuts, it's still safest to give the toasted slivered almonds a quick chop before letting kids eat them.

A Sweet Treat: Chocolate and Asparagus Fondue

TOTAL TIME: 25 minutes PREP:20 minutes COOK: 5 minutes SERVES: 6

I know what you're thinking: "Asparagus in fondue? Seriously?" Yep, seriously. Has your kid made fondue before? After trying this recipe, she might just assume that all fondue is made with asparagus. When kids add even a touch of a vegetable to any dish, vegetables become a staple in the household, and desserts are no exception. Serve this chocolaty mixture in a heated fondue pot or pour it into individual ramekins, and set out fondue forks or small cocktail forks for dipping fruit.

4 thick stalks asparagus
½ cup (120 ml) plus 1 tablespoon coconut milk
1 cup (175 g) dark chocolate chips (60 percent cacao) or semisweet if you prefer a sweeter fondue
1 teaspoon pure vanilla extract
Sliced strawberries and bananas (for dipping)

1 Wash and dry the asparagus, then snap off and discard the woody ends. Peel away any thick outer layer of the stalks. Steam the stalks until they are very soft. Chop into 1-inch (2.5 cm) pieces and pulse these in a blender or food processor until you have an ultrasmooth puree, adding 1 tablespoon of the coconut milk for smooth consistency.

2 Melt the chocolate chips with the remaining ½ cup (120 ml) coconut milk and the vanilla in a double boiler or heated fondue pot and stir in the asparagus puree.

3 Pour the fondue into ramekins if not using a fondue pot. Spear some fruit on a fork and start dipping!

All Kids Can . . .

- Wash and dry the asparagus, snapping off the woody ends
- Chop the cooled asparagus with a kid-safe knife

- Place the ingredients in the blender
- Turn the blender on and off (with adult supervision)

Plus, Big Kids Can . . .

- Peel the asparagus (with adult supervision)

- Steam the asparagus stalks (with adult supervision)
- Melt the fondue ingredients in a double boiler (with adult supervision)

BROCCOLI

Broccoli is loaded with nutrients, including vitamins C, K, A, and B6, calcium, magnesium, potassium, and iron. It even has protein and fiber—it's an amazing powerhouse of nutrition in every bite! Fresh broccoli from a farm stand or grocer should be odorless with tight, green florets that may have a bluish tint. Packages of chopped or frozen broccoli are both terrific time savers, but there is nothing like the flavor of fresh when first introducing this popular vegetable to kids! Broccoli is a cruciferous vegetable and a member of the brassica family, just like cabbage and brussels sprouts.

EXPOSE

Jungle Animals

Creating a jungle of broccoli trees inhabited by monkeys, snakes, and other wild animals makes it hard for your "little monkeys" to resist nibbling on a few branches! Older kids can make more elaborate jungle scenes or a diorama, a three-dimensional action scene captured in a small space, such as a shoe box.

What you'll need:

- 1 large head broccoli, with thick stem intact
- Shallow bin or similar container, at least the size of a shoe box
- Brown rice (uncooked) to fill the bin halfway
- Plastic jungle animals (often sold in inexpensive sets in toy departments)

What to do:

1 KIDS: Pour the brown rice into the bin to a depth of at least 1 inch (2.5 cm). Break apart the head of broccoli into various-sized trees and press them into the rice, creating a jungle scene for playing pretend with the animals.

2 PARENTS AND KIDS: Rinse off the broccoli trees when playtime is over and pat them dry. Place them in a small container with a damp paper towel over the top and set them in the refrigerator vegetable bin to use in the exploration recipes. If a few broccoli trees get eaten in the process, that's just fine!

How your child benefits

As the kids snap apart the "trees" of the broccoli, the nerves in their fingers and palms send signals to the brain to get filed with memories of similar encounters, like breaking apart corn chips or other crunchy foods. If those associations are positive, it increases the likelihood that your child will be open to liking broccoli. As the fingers, hands, and brain work together to understand the tactile properties of this cruciferous vegetable, the brain stores that information in anticipation of that same sensation in the mouth. Playing with food prepares kids for tasting new foods.

Broccoli Tots

TOTAL TIME: 30 minutes PREP: 15 minutes COOK: 12 minutes SERVES: 6

Do you love Food Network programs on TV like I do? My friend Laura Fuentes, founder of MOMables (momables.com) and a winner on Food Network's *Rewrapped*, shared this recipe with me. It's terrific for babies, too—a perfect size for little fists to hold! The potato-broccoli mixture can be stored in the refrigerator for up to three days, if you don't want to use it all at once or you want to make it ahead of time. This recipe calls for a food processor, and although a mini processor will work fine, you may need to divide the recipe in half for pulsing in the smaller bowl of a mini processor. Potatoes and florets can also be chopped very finely by hand, but keep in mind it will take more time.

2 large russet potatoes, peeled and cubed
2 cups (140 g) chopped broccoli florets
2 cups (200 g) shredded Parmesan
1 tablespoon Italian seasoning

❶ Preheat the oven to 425°F (215°C) and place the oven rack in the middle of the oven. Line a baking sheet with parchment paper or a silicone mat to prevent sticking.

❷ Steam the potatoes until they're barely fork tender but too tough to eat (about 10 minutes). Drain and cool.

❸ Pulse the broccoli florets in a food processor until the broccoli resembles coarse rice. Transfer to a large bowl.

❹ Pulse 1 cup (100 g) of the Parmesan with the potatoes in the food processor just enough to create small chunks. Be sure not to overprocess, or you'll have potato glue! Add the mixture to the bowl with the broccoli. Add the Italian seasoning and fold to combine all the ingredients.

❺ Using a tablespoon cookie scoop or your hands, form the seasoned mixture into small balls about ¾ inch (2 cm) in diameter. Roll each nugget in the remaining cheese to coat.

❻ Place the nuggets on a baking sheet ½ to 1 inch (13 mm to 2.5 cm) apart. Bake for 12 minutes or until golden brown.

All Kids Can . . .

- Wash and dry the potatoes and broccoli
- Chop the broccoli with a kid-safe knife
- Add the ingredients to the food processor
- Turn the food processor on and off (with adult supervision)

- Scoop up the seasoned veggie mixture to form nuggets
- Arrange the nuggets on the baking sheet

Plus, Big Kids Can . . .

- Peel the potatoes (with adult supervision)

Broccoli and Cheddar Rice Squares

TOTAL TIME: 45 minutes (not including rice cooking time) PREP: 10 minutes COOK: 35 minutes
SERVES: 6

Don't ever feel like there's anything wrong with using frozen vegetables, including broccoli. I like fresh vegetables for food play and those first introductions, but I quickly move to other options for convenience and to save money. Frozen veggies are packed with nutrition, inexpensive, available year-round, and so easy to keep in your freezer to create a quick, healthy snack. This recipe came from the website fieldsofflavor.com, created by my friend Clancy Cash Harrison, a pediatric registered dietitian. She's a national expert on making healthy foods affordable to all families. She's a big fan of frozen, and I am, too!

1½ cups (235 g) frozen broccoli florets, thawed and drained
2 cups cooked brown rice (390 g) or cooked white rice (370 g)
1 cup (115 g) plus ½ cup (55 g) shredded mild cheddar
4 large eggs, beaten
¼ cup (25 g) dried bread crumbs (gluten-free if needed)
1 teaspoon salt or to taste
1 teaspoon garlic powder

1 Preheat the oven to 350°F (180°C). Generously grease an 8 × 8-inch (20 × 20 cm) baking dish.

2 Chop the broccoli to the desired size and shape—let your child decide what's best!

3 In a large bowl, combine the broccoli, rice, 1 cup (115 g) of the cheddar, the eggs, bread crumbs, salt, and garlic powder. Mix very well to combine.

4 Transfer the mixture to the prepared baking dish. Press the mixture down with a wooden spoon. Sprinkle the casserole with the remaining ½ cup cheese.

5 Cover and bake for 30 minutes or until set. Uncover and cook for another 5 minutes, until browned.

6 Remove from the oven, cool for 10 minutes, and cut into squares.

All Kids Can . . .

- Open any packages that the ingredients came in
- Chop the broccoli with a kid-safe knife
- Beat the eggs
- Mix the ingredients in a bowl
- Help transfer the mixture to the baking dish and press it down with a wooden spoon
- Sprinkle the casserole with cheese

Broccoli and Chicken Enchiladas

TOTAL TIME: 1 hour 15 minutes PREP: 55 minutes COOK: 30 to 35 minutes
SERVES: 4 (two enchiladas each)

Salsa verde (green sauce) is a tangy Mexican staple that blends beautifully with all the flavors in these enchiladas. Start with a mild sauce in a jar, but check the ingredients. If it contains corn syrup or if one of the first three ingredients is sugar, choose another brand. Those cheaper ingredients only make it cheap, not tasty or nutritious. This recipe takes more time than the others in this book, so consider doubling it and making a second baking dish of eight enchiladas for later in the week. Better yet, is there someone in your neighborhood who needs dinner this week? Just imagine how happy they would be if you brought them a homemade meal. Doubling recipes saves time and money, but it also brings kindness door to door.

2 cups (140 g) broccoli florets
1 tablespoon vegetable oil
3 scallions, thinly sliced
One 12-ounce (340 g) jar mild salsa verde
2 cups (250 g) shredded meat from a rotisserie chicken (or see Tip)
2 cups (230 g) shredded cheddar (or replace half of the cheddar with shredded mozzarella)
Juice of 2 limes
Chopped fresh cilantro to taste (a small handful of leaves is my preference!)
Eight 6-inch (15 cm) corn tortillas
½ cup (115 g) sour cream
¼ cup (60 ml) chicken broth

1 Preheat the oven to 350°F (180°C). Grease a 9 × 12-inch (23 × 30 cm) glass or ceramic baking dish.

2 Chop the broccoli florets into whatever size you prefer, or pulse them to rice size in a food processor.

3 In a large skillet, heat the oil over medium-high heat. Sauté the scallions and broccoli until softened. Remove the pan from the heat.

4 In a large bowl, combine ½ cup (120 g) of the salsa verde with the chicken, broccoli, scallions, and half of the cheese.

⑤ In a medium skillet, combine the lime juice and remaining salsa verde and bring to a gentle simmer. Stir in half of the cilantro, then keep the mixture warm over the lowest possible heat.

⑥ Using tongs, place 1 tortilla in the warm salsa verde and heat for 5 seconds to soften. Remove the tortilla and put it on a plate for immediate assembly of an enchilada: Spoon the chicken filling down the center of the tortilla—just enough to spread in a line from one edge to the other. Fold over the empty sides of the tortilla over the center. Place the enchilada seam-side down in the baking dish. Continue dipping, filling, and rolling until the baking dish is filled with eight enchiladas squeezed up next to each other. Do not layer enchiladas on top of each other.

⑦ Add the sour cream and broth to the warm salsa verde, stirring to combine. Pour this sauce evenly over the enchiladas. Cover the baking dish with foil and bake for 15 minutes.

⑧ Remove the foil and top with the remaining cheese and more cilantro. Bake until the cheese is melted, about 5 minutes.

All Kids Can . . .

- Shred the cooked meat
- Chop the broccoli with a kid-safe knife
- Juice the limes
- Chop the cilantro with a kid-safe knife
- Combine the ingredients in a bowl
- Pour the sauce over the enchiladas (with an adult's help)
- Add the final layer of cheese (with an adult's help)

Plus, Big Kids Can . . .

- Sauté the scallions and broccoli (with adult supervision)
- Add ingredients to skillets (with adult supervision)
- Heat the tortillas and spoon the filling mixture to form enchiladas (with adult supervision)

TIP

The juiciest and most tender white-meat chicken results from a wet brine and subsequent roasting. It takes a little more time, but if you prepare more than one breast, the cooked chicken can be used over the next few days in other recipes. In a large bowl, dissolve ¼ cup (75 g) salt in 1 quart (1 L) water. Place two or three boneless, skinless chicken breasts in a large freezer bag and set on a cutting board. Using a wooden mallet or rolling pin, pound the breasts to flatten them to an even thickness. Remove the breasts, discard the plastic bag, and submerge the meat in the brine. Cover the bowl with plastic wrap and place in the refrigerator for 30 minutes.

Preheat the oven to 450°F (230°C). Remove the breasts, discard the brine, and lightly pat the meat dry with a paper towel. Season both sides with salt and pepper. Place the breasts in a small baking dish coated with cooking spray, with space in between for even cooking, and cook for about 20 minutes, until the internal temperature reaches 165°F (75°C). Remove from the oven and let rest for 5 minutes before using in a recipe. Store whole breasts in the refrigerator for up to four days and wait to slice them just prior to adding to another recipe to ensure moistness.

PARENTING IN THE KITCHEN

If your child is a more hesitant eater, go for ricing the broccoli instead of using chopped florets. He'll still eat the same amount of broccoli; it's just not as obvious with each bite. Remember, the important thing is that they help you make the enchiladas with broccoli—it's not about hiding vegetables.

A Sweet Treat: Chase Yur Dreams Ice Pops

TOTAL TIME: 3 to 5 hours PREP: 5 minutes MAKES: 6 to 8 ice pops

Chase Bailey is a teenager who ate only five foods as a toddler, until he became interested in cooking. His mother, Mary, encouraged Chase to follow his dreams to become a top chef, and today, he's appeared with celebrity chefs on national TV, plus he has his own cookbook (*The Official Chase 'N Yur Face Cookbook*)! He's one cool kid who also has autism, making the sensory aspects of cooking exceptionally challenging, but he did it! Chase created this frozen sweet treat, and I'm proud to include it in this book. Check out his website at chasenyurface.com.

1 cup (70 g) broccoli florets
1 cup (100 g) chopped red cabbage
1 cup (150 g) frozen mango chunks
1½ cups (360 ml) apple juice

Combine all the ingredients in a food processor (or high-powered blender), mixing on high for 1 minute or until smooth. Pour into six to eight ice pop molds. Place in the freezer for 3 to 5 hours, until frozen.

All Kids Can . . .

- Remove outer leaves of cabbage and chop using a kid-safe knife
- Combine the ingredients in the food processor (with an adult's help)
- Turn the processor on and off (with adult supervision)
- Pour the blend into ice pop molds (with an adult's help)

CARROTS

Vitamin A (beta-carotene) won't give us X-ray eyes, but the beta-carotene and lutein in carrots is still fantastic for top-notch vision! Carrots come in all sizes, shapes, and colors. Baby carrots are simply made by machines from large orange carrots, perfectly crafted into smooth tubular pieces and packed in a bag with a touch of water to keep them fresh. Larger carrots are sometimes advertised as "rainbow carrots," which can come in white, yellow, purple, and of course orange. Whatever the color, like many root vegetables, they become sweeter after enduring a frost. There's something very satisfying about growing carrots. Take a bucket of water out to the garden and let your kids pull up a beautiful carrot and dunk it straight in the water to wash. There's really no need to peel or cut it for kids over age three—just snap off and discard the tip and take a crunch while standing in the soil.

EXPOSE
Carrot Crunch Contest

Get the family together (or some of your kids' friends), let them choose a carrot, and find out . . . who can crunch one the loudest! This is an ideal game for a child who is hesitant to take a bite of raw carrots. They can just bite and crunch, then place the piece on their plate without eating it, and still win the game!

You can use an app on your cell phone or computer that reads decibels if you want to raise the stakes on this activity. The voice recorder on most cell phones will also work because it provides a visual image of the rise and fall of sound. Otherwise, choose one person to be the judge to determine who crunched the loudest.

What you'll need:

- Baby carrots, full-size carrots, or both—as long as there's one for everybody! (For kids under the age of three, offer the smallest baby carrots in the bag, for safety reasons.)

What to do:

1 KIDS: Wash and peel the carrots, cutting off the tips of full-size carrots, which can be stringy.

2 PARENTS AND KIDS: Each person chooses a carrot and takes a turn giving it one loud crunch!

3 PARENTS: Have someone be the judge (or use the app on a phone): Who crunched the loudest?

4 CHECK IT OUT: What happens if we bite with our front teeth instead of our back teeth? What's the crunch difference between biting a narrow piece of carrot compared to biting a wider piece? What happens if you bite a small piece, close your lips, and crunch?

How your child benefits

Learning to try a new food involves all our senses, even hearing. Discovering the sound of carrots in our mouth introduces our brain to an important sensory component of many raw vegetables—the crunch!

KITCHEN SCIENCE

Why can we hear the crunch, if our mouth is closed? To encourage chewing and swallowing in kids over age three, show your child how to bite off a *small* piece of carrot, place it on the molars, and chew hard while closing each ear canal with a finger. When you plug your ears, can you still hear the crunch? Sound waves don't just travel through the air; they travel via bone conduction, too! So when you crunch on a carrot with your mouth closed, the sound you're hearing is traveling to the inner ear via the bones in your face and skull.

Honey-Butter Carrots with Dill

TOTAL TIME: 10 minutes PREP: 2 minutes COOK: 6 to 8 minutes SERVES: 4 to 6

This simple recipe is so easy to make that you'll find you're serving it often. That's the key: Keep preparing vegetables with your kids, continue presenting vegetables for snacks and mealtimes, and make vegetables a familiar staple on your family's plates. The only way to make friends with veggies is to have them hang out with your family as much as possible.

1 pound (455 g) baby carrots
2 tablespoons (30 g) salted butter
2 tablespoons honey
1 tablespoon chopped fresh dill (or substitute 1 teaspoon dried dill)

❶ Put the baby carrots in a medium saucepan and pour in just enough water to cover them. Bring the water to a boil, cover the pan, and reduce the heat to a simmer. Cook the carrots until they're fork tender but not too soft, then drain.

❷ Return the carrots to the hot pan and add the butter, stirring to melt. Add the honey, stirring until dissolved.

❸ Sprinkle dill over the carrots. If your child is hesitant about dill, hold back on the amount of garnish and just put the extra dill on a small dish on the table when you serve the carrots, in case anyone would like to add more.

PARENTING IN THE KITCHEN

Helping kids tend to an herb garden on your windowsill is a brilliant way to introduce new aromas and flavors to kids. Start with dill, basil, and peppermint. Kids love to rub the leaves between their fingers, releasing the oils and aroma. You'll be surprised how often kids will take a taste of an herb, even though it's that dreaded color: green! As an added plus, research shows that kids who participate in gardening (yes, even windowsill gardens!) are likely to score higher in science achievement tests, because it sparks an interest in how things grow and other facts about nature and science.

All Kids Can . . .

- Place the baby carrots in the pan and add water
- Add the butter and honey to the carrots and stir to melt (with an adult's help)
- Sprinkle the dill over the carrots

Carrot Latkes

TOTAL TIME: 30 minutes PREP: 20 minutes COOK: 3 minutes per batch
MAKES: about twelve 3-inch (7.5 cm) latkes

Loaded with shredded carrots, these latkes make a terrific finger food for kids of all ages, even babies! Latkes are often served with applesauce or sour cream for dipping or topping, but plain or low-sugar flavored yogurt makes a good dip, too. (Or you can add a touch of applesauce to plain yogurt to sweeten it naturally.) The best potatoes for latkes are russets, because they have a higher starch content and are less likely to fall apart while cooking. No need to peel them—keep all the skin in place for some added fiber.

2 or 3 carrots, peeled and shredded
1 medium russet potato, shredded
2 large scallions, finely sliced
2 or 3 large eggs, beaten
1 or 2 tablespoons all-purpose flour (for a gluten-free option, try coconut or chickpea flour)
½ teaspoon salt
Vegetable oil as needed for the skillet
Sour cream, applesauce, or yogurt for dipping (optional)

1 In a large bowl, combine 2 carrots, the potato, scallions, 2 eggs, 1 tablespoon flour, and salt, reserving the extra carrot, egg, and flour to add after sampling the first latke, if needed.

2 Heat oil in a large skillet over medium-high heat. Drop a heaping tablespoon of the latke mix into the pan, flattening it with the back of a spoon or spatula into a pancake shape. Cook for 2 to 3 minutes, flipping once, until the latke is cooked through and both sides are golden brown.

3 Remove the latke and place it on paper towel to soak up some of the oil. When it's cool enough to sample, taste-test by taking a bite. Does it need more carrot? More flour or egg to help hold it together? If so, add whatever seems needed. Cook the remaining latkes

2 inches (5 cm) apart in the skillet. Add oil to the pan as needed as you go along, and drain the cooked latkes on a paper towel after removing from the skillet.

④ Serve accompanied by sour cream, applesauce, or yogurt, if desired.

All Kids Can . . .

- Wash and dry the potato and the carrots
- Mix the ingredients together

Big Kids Can . . .

- Peel the carrots (with adult supervision)
- Shred the potato and carrots (with adult supervision)

- Slice the scallions with a sharp knife (with adult supervision) or using a cat paw (see page 65)
- Cook the latkes (with adult supervision)

PARENTING IN THE KITCHEN

It bears repeating: Encourage taste testing whenever you can. In this latke recipe, we are testing for texture; in other recipes, we are tasting for a balance of flavors. When kids taste and adjust the recipe as needed, it gives them confidence in their ability to create something that perfectly suits their palate.

Deviled Carrot Eggs

TOTAL TIME: 25 minutes plus 1 hour of refrigeration afterward (not including egg boiling time)
PREP: 20 minutes MAKES: 16 deviled eggs

The natural sweetness of the carrots combined with the tang of Greek yogurt makes this healthy version of deviled eggs tempting for hesitant eaters. Add just a touch of filling to each egg at first, gradually adding more filling with each serving, once your child gets used to the texture.

3 medium to large carrots, peeled and sliced into coins about ½ inch (13 mm) thick
8 hard-boiled eggs (see Tip on cooking easy-to-peel eggs)
½ cup (140 g) plain 2 percent Greek yogurt
1 tablespoon mayonnaise (omit for babies under the age of 1 year)
1 tablespoon white balsamic vinegar
1 teaspoon dried dill
½ teaspoon Dijon mustard
½ teaspoon smoked paprika, plus more for garnish if desired
Salt and black pepper to taste
Sea salt to garnish

1 Steam the carrots until they're fork tender and drain. Then puree them in a high-powered blender or food processor.

2 Peel the hard-boiled eggs (see Tip) and cut them in half lengthwise. Scoop out the yolks.

3 Add the egg yolks, yogurt, mayonnaise, vinegar, dill, and paprika to the carrot puree and blend until smooth. Season with salt and pepper.

4 Using a pastry bag or a small spoon, add a teensy dollop of the carrot filling to the center of each egg white—or pilc it high, if your kids already love traditional deviled eggs.

⑤ Sprinkle the deviled eggs with paprika for garnish, if desired, and sprinkle with sea salt for a touch of crunch—kids like that!

⑥ Cover the eggs and refrigerate for at least an hour for optimal flavor before serving. Use any remaining filling for dipping crudités or buttery crackers (see page 81 for more about crudités).

All Kids Can . . .

- Hard-boil the eggs (with an adult's help)
- Chop the carrots with a kid-safe knife
- Put the carrots in the blender and turn the blender on and off (with adult supervision)
- Peel the hard-boiled eggs
- Cut the eggs in half and remove the yolks
- Mix the egg yolks with the creamy and spicy ingredients to make the filling
- Add salt and pepper to the filling mixture as needed

- Fill the whites of the hard-boiled eggs with the yolk mixture
- Garnish with paprika

Plus, Big Kids Can . . .

- Peel the carrots (with adult supervision)
- Steam the carrots

 TIP

The secret to cooking hard-boiled eggs that are easy to peel is . . . vinegar! Vinegar breaks down calcium, and eggshells are made of calcium carbonate. If you add vinegar to your egg-boiling water, it will eat away at the shell while the egg is cooking, making it easier to peel. So try this foolproof method for easy-to-peel eggs: Add 1 tablespoon salt and 2 tablespoons vinegar to a large pot of water, cover, and heat on medium. Before the water reaches a boil, slip in up to a dozen large eggs. Replace the cover and boil for 2 minutes, then turn off the heat and let the eggs sit in the hot water, covered, for 11 more minutes. Drain the eggs and allow them to cool slightly before peeling.

PARENTING IN THE KITCHEN

The creamy carrot and egg filling makes an ideal first food for babies, as do the plain boiled eggs. The American Academy of Pediatrics recommends that both the white and the yolk be cooked thoroughly and offered to babies as young as six months, but no earlier. Because baby's iron stores begin to deplete after six months of age, eggs offer iron plus protein—two essential building blocks for growth.

A Sweet Treat: Tropical Carrot Confetti Cookies

TOTAL TIME: 45 minutes PREP: 25 minutes COOK: 18 to 20 minutes MAKES: 2 dozen cookies

The soft texture of these cookies is like a muffin top, which everyone knows is the best part of a muffin! Three large rainbow carrots chopped into tiny pieces of colorful confetti make these cookies a crowd-pleaser. Not only that, but they also offer an extra nutritional boost from one of my favorite add-ins: hemp seeds.

2 teaspoons coconut oil

3 large carrots, in three colors (for instance, purple, orange, and yellow) if available

1 cup (125 g) all-purpose flour (gluten-free if needed)

1 cup (90 g) old-fashioned rolled oats (gluten-free if needed)

1 teaspoon baking soda

½ teaspoon salt

¼ teaspoon ground cinnamon

6 tablespoons (90 g) unsalted butter, at room temperature

½ cup (100 g) firmly packed light brown sugar

½ cup (110 g) banana puree (made from one large ripe banana; freeze any leftover for future use)

½ cup (120 g) pineapple puree (made from pieces of drained canned pineapple or from frozen pineapple chunks that have been thawed in the microwave and drained)

½ cup (80 g) raisins

½ cup (60 g) chopped walnuts

¼ cup (20 g) unsweetened shredded coconut

2 tablespoons hemp seeds

2 packets (about 2 teaspoons) raw sugar (optional; see Tip)

① Preheat the oven to 350°F (180°C). Warm the oil between clean hands, then rub 1 teaspoon over the surface of each of two baking sheets. The coconut oil gives a subtle tropical flavor and crisp to the bottom of the cookie.

② Break each carrot into several pieces. Using a mini food processor or a high-powered blender made for chopping, chop each carrot separately, emptying the pieces into three separate bowls. If a few pieces of each color remain in the processor, that's fine, but chop the purple carrot last, so that the purple remnants won't stain the lighter carrot pieces.

❸ In a medium bowl, combine the flour, oats, baking soda, salt, and cinnamon.

❹ In a large bowl, mash the butter and sugar with clean hands until well combined. Stir in the banana and pineapple with your hands or a wooden spoon. Add the flour mixture and mix gently with your hands or a spoon until just combined. Don't overstir, or the muffins will come out chewy! Gently fold in the carrots, raisins, walnuts, coconut, and hemp seeds.

❺ Drop the dough by the heaping tablespoonful (or use a large melon baller for consistency) onto the baking sheets, 1 inch (2.5 cm) apart, slightly flattening each one. Sprinkle the top of the flattened dough balls with just a touch of raw sugar, if desired.

❻ Bake for 18 to 20 minutes, until lightly browned.

❼ Cool on a cooling rack.

All Kids Can . . .

- Puree pineapple and banana (with an adult's help)
- Prep the baking sheets with oil
- Wash and dry the carrots
- Break the carrots or chop with a kid-safe knife
- Put the carrots into the food processor (with an adult's help)
- Combine the dry ingredients
- Mash the butter and sugar with clean hands
- Combine the wet ingredients
- Fold in the raisins, walnuts, coconut, and hemp seeds
- Use a spoon or melon baller to drop the dough onto the baking sheet
- Sprinkle the balls of dough with raw sugar

Plus, Big Kids Can . . .

- Peel the carrots (with adult supervision)

 TIP

I always save packets of raw sugar that come with my drive-through coffee runs, even though I don't add sugar to my coffee. Just one packet sprinkled on top of a dozen muffins gives the top a sparkly sheen and a sweet crunch without adding tons more sugar.

PEAS

Peas have protein for muscles and are loaded with B-vitamins to keep our heart healthy. Plus, they have loads of fiber, which contributes to heart health. Sugar snap peas, snow peas, or traditional English peas— there so many to choose from, and they are all so tasty! Did you know that snow peas, sometimes called Chinese pea pods (thanks to their prevalence in Asian cooking), are called *mange-tout* in French? It means "eat all" because you can eat the whole vegetable—pod and all. I personally love peas and eat all that I can, but I'm not a fan of telling kids to eat all of *their* vegetables, even peas. Kids—not adults—get to decide how much they eat. Our job is just to help them learn to love healthy foods by following the Three *E*'s and presenting healthy options to them on a consistent basis. It's their job to listen to their bodies and decide when they are full. Teach mindful eating.

EXPOSE

Pea-Shelling Contest

Who can shell peas the fastest? Warning: A few peas (as well as the tasty edible pods themselves) may go missing when your kids pop a few right into their mouths.

What you'll need:

- Fresh sugar snap peas, which have tasty, edible pods (English shelling peas can be eaten raw, but the pods are too stringy and fibrous to be eaten)
- Bowls

What to do:

1 KIDS: Rinse and dry the sugar snap peas.

2 PARENTS AND KIDS: Everyone gets a bowl and one person sets the timer. Ready, set, go! Pop open the pods and shell peas into the bowl until the timer rings, as fast as you can. The one with the most peas wins!

3 PARENTS: Explain to younger kids how some pea pods hold more peas than others. Which ones are best for winning this game: the bigger pods or the smaller ones? Encourage different methods of counting and categorizing. Can your school-age child count by twos or threes? Can toddlers separate the peas by size?

How your child benefits

Playing with food isn't just good for the belly, it's good for the brain. You'll find myriad ways to teach math, science, and language skills as you progress through the activities in this book. The examples here include addition (math), categorization (language), and observation of how pea pods grow to different sizes (science). The purpose of these exercises is to get you and your child to think about food in a different way. What other ways could you play with peas? How about using the pods to make letters or pretending the pods are canoes traveling the Nile River?

Pea and Avocado Dip

TOTAL TIME: 10 minutes PREP: 10 minutes MAKES: about 1½ cups (340 g)

Keep this basic guacamole simple, flavored with just lime and salt—or make it zestier by using one of the suggested spice combinations. You can make a dip that's chunky with avocado pieces or blend everything until it's creamy and smooth. Serve with raw veggies, pita chips, or tortilla chips.

1 large ripe avocado
1 cup (150 g) frozen peas, thawed
Juice of 1 lime
Salt to taste

OPTIONAL SPICE COMBO 1

¼ cup (5 g) finely chopped fresh cilantro
2 scallions, sliced finely
1 garlic clove, chopped

OPTIONAL SPICE COMBO 2

1 teaspoon adobo seasoning
1 garlic clove, chopped

OPTIONAL SPICE COMBO 3

6 large fresh mint leaves, finely chopped
1 garlic clove, chopped

❶ Cut the avocado in half, remove the pit, and scoop out the flesh. (Cut the flesh into chunks and reserve to add after everything else is blended, if you prefer chunky guacamole.)

❷ Combine the peas, avocado (unless you're adding chunks later), and lime juice in the bowl of a food processor. Add optional spices (if using). Pulse to the desired consistency—for chunkier dip, remove half of the mixture midway through the processing and stir it back in before serving, or stir chunks of avocado into the mix after processing all the other ingredients. Season with salt to taste.

All Kids Can . . .

- Slice the avocado with a kid-safe knife
- Scoop out the avocado flesh

- Juice the lime
- Cut any herbs (if using) with kid-safe kitchen shears (see page 259)
- Put the ingredients in the food processor and pulse them (with an adult's help)

Three *P*'s in a Pod Pasta

TOTAL TIME: 30 minutes PREP: 10 minutes COOK: 20 minutes SERVES: 6 as an entrée, plus extra peas for another day

Save some of the sautéed peas from this recipe to serve as a side dish on Saturday or Sunday. (Can your kids say that five times fast?) Of course, any day will do!

2 cups (170 g) penne pasta (gluten-free if needed)
2 tablespoons olive oil
2 cups (150 g) sugar snap peas
1 cup (150 g) English peas (or frozen peas, slightly thawed)
1 cup (230 g) pesto (store-bought is fine)
Salt and black pepper to taste
1 cup (100 g) shredded Pecorino Romano or Parmesan

1 Boil a pot of water and cook the pasta as directed on the package.

2 While the pasta is cooking, heat the olive oil in a large skillet over medium heat. Add the sugar snap peas and sauté for 4 to 5 minutes, until tender-crisp. Add the English peas and sauté for 2 minutes more. Remove half of the pea mixture to serve on the side of the pasta or to refrigerate for another day.

3 Turn off the heat, add the pesto to the remaining peas in the saucepan, and stir to warm. Cover until you're ready to add the pasta.

4 Once the pasta is al dente, drain and stir it into the pea mixture. Season with salt and pepper.

5 Serve topped with the cheese.

PARENTING IN THE KITCHEN

As Kermit the Frog said, "It's not easy being green." Kids seem to quickly turn their noses up at green food, so many parents stop serving it. The trick is to *keep serving green*. Make the whole dish green (like Three *P*'s in a Pod Pasta) or present it as a side dish with another preferred food. Encourage kids to celebrate green and find as many green things as they can to decorate the table. Green plates, green tablecloth, green candles, green napkins . . . go green!

All Kids Can . . .

- Wash and dry the sugar snap peas
- Spread the frozen peas (if used) out to thaw
- Add salt and pepper to taste
- Top the pasta with shredded cheese

Plus, Big Kids Can . . .

- Cook the pasta (with adult supervision)
- Sauté the peas (with adult supervision)
- Combine the pasta and peas with the pesto

Comforting Curry with Pineapple and Peas

TOTAL TIME: **35** minutes PREP: 20 minutes COOK: 15 minutes SERVES: 8 with leftovers

This quick and simple curry is an adaption of a recipe created by the Colorado chef Ben Chansingthong. When my first book was published a few years ago, Ben was still in cooking school and he catered my book party. Today, in collaboration with his family, he owns three different restaurants! I was honored to help create the kid's menu for his first restaurant, Urban Thai. Each "kid's meal" at Urban Thai is a fun variation of the adult menu, but in kid-size portions. Every single one comes with fresh veggies for dipping in Thai sauce.

2 tablespoons coconut oil

¼ cup (80 g) red curry paste

2 chicken breasts, flattened and chopped into 1-inch (2.5 cm) pieces (see Parenting in the Kitchen), or one 16-ounce (454 g) package firm tofu, chopped into 1-inch (2.5 cm) cubes

One or two 13.5-ounce (398 ml) cans unsweetened coconut milk

1 or 2 cans water (use the empty coconut milk can)

1 cup (135g) frozen peas or 12 fresh snow pea pods, washed and trimmed

½ to 1 cup (80 to 165 g) pineapple, fresh or canned and drained, in bite-sized chunks (use the amount you prefer)

1 tablespoon sliced lemongrass (optional)

2 tablespoons sugar

6 tablespoons fish sauce

4 cups cooked white rice (635 g) or cooked brown rice (780 g) (see Tip)

❶ Heat the oil in large saucepan over medium-high heat. Add the red curry paste and warm until aromatic. Add the chicken and stir occasionally for about 4 minutes, until the chicken is cooked through.

❷ Add one can of the coconut milk and stir to mix well. Let the coconut milk mixture come to a boil and boil for 3 to 4 minutes. Add one can of water and, if needed, the second can of coconut milk and water, stirring well. Add the peas, pineapple, and lemongrass (if using) and bring the

mixture to a boil. Boil for 5 to 6 minutes, then turn off the heat to allow it to cool a bit.

③ Add half of the sugar and half of the fish sauce, stirring well. Taste-test the liquid (allow it to cool slightly on a spoon) and add more sugar and/or fish sauce as desired. Bring the curry back to a boil, then turn off the heat. Remove the lemongrass, if using.

④ Serve the curry over warm rice. To mold the rice into fun shapes, help your child hold a cookie cutter on a plate while you spoon rice into the middle. Pat firmly and keep filling with rice until molded as desired. Carefully lift up the cutter

to reveal a shape ready for curry to be spooned on top!

All Kids Can . . .

- Pass ingredients to the chef, except for the raw meat
- Snip the lemongrass (if using) with kid-safe kitchen shears (see page 259)
- Make rice shapes for each bowl of curry, using cookie cutters

Plus, Big Kids Can . . .

- Flatten the chicken breasts (see Parenting in the Kitchen for safe meat handling tips)
- Heat the oil and add ingredients according to the directions (with adult supervision)

Wonder why some kids don't like to eat rice? Some types of rice can be frustrating to keep on a fork and crumble around the tongue—that can feel tickly! Sticky rice solves that problem, especially when molded into enticing shapes with large cookie cutters. If you can't find sticky rice (usually labeled "sweet rice" or "glutinous rice" in Asian groceries), try using short-grain rice such as sushi rice and consider soaking it from 30 minutes to 4 hours before cooking. Also, cooked rice that has been sitting longer can get stickier, so try letting it rest a while before serving or make it a day or two ahead of time (but make sure to cover it in the fridge so it doesn't dry out or spoil). You may also want to grease the food cutter with a little oil before shaping the rice. Let the kids spoon as much of the curry as they like over sticky, warm rice in a favorite shape. The extra moisture in the rice makes it easier to eat, is more flavorful, and provides the mouthfeel that many kids crave.

PARENTING IN THE KITCHEN

Foodborne bacteria can cause serious illness, especially in children. Keep younger kids away from raw meat entirely, and teach older children safe handling and cleaning techniques for working with raw meat. Use hot soapy water to wash any utensil, cutting board, plates, or counters that may have come in contact with the uncooked meat. Use a separate cutting board and knife for preparing uncooked meats and another knife and cutting board for slicing meats once they are cooked. Never put cooked meat on a platter that once held raw meat (for instance, when grilling)— always transfer the cooked meat to a clean dish. Keep raw meat away from all other foods and from kids' hands until they are old enough to understand the importance of these safe handling techniques, as well as how to keep their hands away from their face and away from other foods when they're handling raw meat.

A Sweet Treat: Give Peas a Chance Cake

TOTAL TIME: I hour 20 minutes PREP: 20 minutes COOK: 45 to 60 minutes SERVES: 8 to 12

This ultramoist cake has a lemony tang and two whole cups of peas! It's my go-to cake to bring to a new neighbor or anyone who needs a little extra love. It's my most requested recipe and I'm happy to share it here with you.

2 cups (275 g) frozen peas, thawed
¾ cup (170 g) unsalted butter, at room temperature
¾ cup (150 g) plus ⅓ cup (65 g) sugar
3 large eggs
2 teaspoons pure vanilla extract
Zest and juice of ½ lemon, plus juice of 1 whole lemon for glaze
2 cups (250 g) all-purpose flour (gluten-free if needed)
2 teaspoons baking powder (gluten-free if needed)
½ teaspoon salt
¼ cup (60 ml) buttermilk

❶ Preheat the oven to 325°F (160°C) and grease an 8 × 8-inch (20 × 20 cm) glass pan.

❷ Pulse the thawed peas in a high-powered blender or a food processor until the puree is smooth but still has occasional bits of pea here and there. This makes for a prettier cake after baking!

❸ Cream the butter and ¾ cup (150 g) sugar in a large bowl with an electric mixer or by hand. Beat in the eggs, one at a time. Gently beat in the pea puree, vanilla, and the zest and juice of ½ lemon.

④ Sift the flour, baking powder, and salt together into the bowl and stir gently to combine. Gently stir in the buttermilk.

⑤ Pour the mixture into the greased pan and bake for 45 to 50 minutes. The sides of the cake will brown slightly. Test the center for doneness with a toothpick, which should come out clean.

⑥ Mix the remaining ⅓ cup (65 g) sugar with the juice of 1 lemon to create a runny paste. While the cake is still warm, poke 20 to 25 holes 1 inch (2.5 cm) deep into the cake with a thick toothpick or a wooden skewer. Drizzle the paste over the entire surface, spreading lightly to ensure that the paste seeps into each hole.

⑦ Cut into squares and serve warm or at room temperature.

All Kids Can . . .

- Grease the glass pan
- Puree peas in the blender or food processor (with an adult's help)
- Test for doneness with a toothpick (and with an adult's help)

Plus, Big Kids Can . . .

- Zest and juice the lemon
- Cream the butter and sugar, using an electric mixer (with adult supervision)
- Add the puree and other ingredients to the bowl
- Pour the mixture into the pan

SPINACH

Every time I buy a large package of prewashed spinach at the grocers, I immediately freeze half of it. Using pint-sized freezer bags, I mark each with the date of purchase and put a handful of spinach in each. It's a convenient way to give your recipes a boost of nutrients—spinach is packed full of nutrition superheroes that keep our bones strong, our blood rich in iron, and our heart healthy. Just crumble the frozen leaves right into whatever is on the menu for that day, like scrambled eggs, smoothies, meat loaf, soups, or a stew. Frozen spinach lasts up to six months.

EXPOSE

Magic Spinach Game

Can you guess how much fresh spinach it will take to fill a tiny cup? How about cooked spinach?

What you'll need:

- 10 ounces (285 g) fresh spinach leaves
- Teacup or similar small cup
- 2 teaspoons olive oil
- Sauté pan
- Spatula

What to do:

1 KIDS: Wash and spin or pat dry the spinach if it's not prewashed. One at a time, pack as many leaves of spinach into the teacup as you can, recording how many leaves fit inside.

2 PARENTS AND KIDS: Sauté those leaves in olive oil, let them cool, and place them back in the tea cup.

3 CHECK IT OUT: How much space is left for more spinach? How many more leaves do you think will fill the cup? What's the best way to determine this? Once you've made your hypothesis, sauté those leaves and add them to the cup. Were you correct?

KITCHEN SCIENCE

Why do fresh greens, like spinach, get so much smaller when cooked? Greens are very high in moisture, and as heat causes the cells of the leaves to break down, the moisture evaporates; the remaining parts of the leaf wilt, as it collapses in on itself. It seems like magic, but it's just more kitchen science!

How your child benefits

This simple activity includes math, science, and problem solving. No matter what the age, kids always seem fascinated by this experiment. Older kids may enjoy going online to find some science experiments that include spinach or other plants, where they can learn about photosynthesis and plant DNA. I highly recommend stevespanglerscience.com for science activities that are teacher developed and kid tested. Spangler is a frequent guest on *The Ellen DeGeneres Show*, where he takes classroom science experiments to the extreme, and his kitchen science lessons are fascinating for kids and adults alike.

Polka-Dot Green Dragon Smoothie

TOTAL TIME: 10 minutes SERVES: 4 to 6

In my book *Raising a Healthy, Happy Eater* (coauthored with my pal, the pediatrician Nimali Fernando, aka Doctor Yum), we shared Doctor Yum's recipe for a Green Dragon Smoothie, but I've added a polka-dot twist! (You can find other Doctor Yum recipes at the Doctor Yum Project website: doctoryum.org/the-doctor-yum-project.)

2 cups (45 g) fresh baby spinach, packed
1½ cups (250 g) fresh or frozen chopped pineapple
1 cup (140 g) fresh or frozen green grapes (see Tip)
1 fresh or frozen orange, peeled
½ fresh or frozen banana, peeled
1 lime wedge, with rind, seeds removed
One ¼-inch (6 mm) piece ginger
Ice for desired consistency (optional if using frozen fruit)
¼ cup (60 g) mini chocolate chips

❶ Blend all the ingredients except the chocolate chips in a high-powered blender until they're smooth, adding a splash of water as needed if using all frozen fruit.

❷ Add the chocolate chips and blend for just a few seconds, to create polka dots throughout.

All Kids Can . . .

- Peel the orange and banana
- Put the ingredients in the blender (with an adult's help)
- Slice the ginger with a kid-safe knife

When fresh grapes, oranges, and bananas are on the verge of becoming overripe, wash and freeze by the cupful in freezer bags for using in smoothies! Dry packing is the simplest method. Fill pint-sized freezer bags with washed grapes, peeled orange segments, or chunks of peeled bananas, with just enough fruit so that it lays flat on a freezer shelf in a single layer inside the bag. Leave 1 inch (2.5 cm) of room at the top of the bag so that you can seal the bag with ease and because the fruit will expand slightly as it freezes. Once the fruit is frozen, you can stack the bags or hang them in a row from a wire shelf with mini metal binder clips from the office supply store, just like hangers in your closet!

Sweet Spinach Frittata

TOTAL TIME: 40 minutes PREP: 20 minutes COOK: 20 minutes SERVES: 4 to 6

The sautéed red onions in this all-in-one-pan dish give it a touch of sweetness. If your child already enjoys vegetables, try adding extras such as sautéed mushrooms, red bell pepper, or zucchini. This recipe serves as the foundation to create your favorite frittata.

4 tablespoons olive oil
1 small red onion, chopped
2 garlic cloves, finely chopped
2 cups (45 g) fresh baby spinach
Salt and black pepper to taste
6 large eggs
¼ cup (25 g) grated mild cheddar
¼ cup (25 g) grated Asiago, Parmesan, or Pecorino Romano (see Tip)

1 Preheat the oven to 350°F (180°C) and position the top rack so that it's just slightly higher than the middle of the oven.

2 Chop the spinach in a food processor, reserving 6 to 8 leaves for garnish, if desired.

3 In a medium oven-safe skillet (cast iron is ideal), heat 1 tablespoon of the oil over medium to medium-high heat. Stir in the onion, coating evenly, and cook until translucent. Add the garlic and cook for 1 minute more. Add the spinach, salt, and pepper and sauté until wilted. Transfer all the sautéed ingredients to a few paper towels on a plate, gently squeeze out the extra moisture from the spinach, and throw away the wet paper towels. Cover the vegetables to keep them warm.

4 In a medium bowl, beat the eggs. Stir in the cheddar and the spinach mixture.

5 Add the remaining 3 tablespoons oil to the pan and heat over medium-high heat. Carefully add the egg mixture and reduce the heat to medium. The mixture will begin to set around the edges of your pan but will still appear very wet in the center.

6 Carefully place the pan in the oven. Bake for 8 minutes and then sprinkle the Asiago on top. Continue to bake for up to 5 minutes more. Aim for a lightly browned surface and a frittata that is the consistency of custard. Overcooking will create a sponge-like interior. The frittata will continue to cook in the hot pan once removed from the oven and will look beautiful placed on a trivet on the table.

7 Once the frittata has cooled slightly, you can simply cut it into pie slices, garnish with the reserved whole spinach leaves (if desired), and serve. If you'd prefer to remove the whole frittata from the pan, place a large heat-safe plate over the top of the pan, invert, and the entire frittata will slip right out onto the plate.

All Kids Can . . .

- Crack and beat the eggs
- Shred the cheese if using a safety glove
- Hand the chef other ingredients
- Add the cheese to the top of the frittata (with an adult's help)

Plus, Big Kids Can . . .

- Chop the onion and garlic with a sharp knife (with adult supervision)
- Sauté the onions, garlic, and spinach (with adult supervision)
- Add the egg mixture (with adult supervision) to the pan and carefully place it in the oven

TIP

What's the difference between Asiago, Parmesan, and Romano cheeses? Asiago is mild and moister than the other two and is made from cow's milk. Parmesan is mild and hard and made from unpasteurized cow's milk. Pecorino Romano is made from sheep's milk and has more of a sharpness to it, compared to the other two. What do they all have in common? They taste great with eggs, so pick your favorite or mix a few together!

Tea Sandwiches with Spinach Cream Cheese

TOTAL TIME: 10 minutes MAKES: 8 to 16 finger sandwiches

Traditional English tea sandwiches include paper-thin cucumbers and a touch of cream cheese layered between two pieces of crustless white bread. This healthier version adds finely chopped baby spinach on whole wheat, but if your child only eats white for now, that's OK, too! Be sure to use your fanciest tea cups and wear your best hat or "topper" to make this tea party extra special. Hold out your pinky finger as you drink—it's required at tea parties.

1 cup (20 g) fresh baby spinach

4 ounces (115 g) cream cheese, at room temperature

8 slices whole wheat, white, or gluten-free bread

½ English cucumber, peeled and sliced into thin strips or rounds

1 Chop the spinach in a food processor for the desired consistency. This is a personal preference—to me, pea-sized seems ideal.

2 In a medium bowl, mix the spinach and cream cheese with an electric mixer or by hand.

3 Spread a thin layer of the cream cheese mixture on all the slices of bread.

4 Arrange the cucumber slices in a layer on four of the bread slices, dividing the cucumber evenly. Top with the other four bread slices, cream-cheese side down, to make a sandwich. (The cream cheese should hold the cucumber in place inside the sandwiches.)

5 Cut the crusts off the sandwiches, then cut each sandwich into small triangles, squares, or rectangles and serve.

All Kids Can . . .

- Peel the cucumbers using safety gloves (with an adult's help)
- Place the spinach in the food processor (with an adult's help)
- Pulse the spinach to the desired consistency (with an adult's help)
- Mix the spinach with the cream cheese (with an adult's help if using an electric mixer)

- Slice the cucumbers with a kid-safe knife
- Spread the cream cheese
- Assemble the sandwiches
- Cut the sandwiches into shapes with a kid-safe knife or FunBites food cutters

A Sweet Treat: Chocolate Pudding Surprise

TOTAL TIME: 1 hour PREP: 15 minutes MAKES: 4 to 6 pudding cups

Kids will love finding a sweet surprise in the center of each pudding cup! What they won't be surprised about is the full cup of spinach used in this recipe. When kids are active participants in the kitchen, they become comfortable with all sorts of ingredients. Spinach can show up in lots of different recipes–even in a dessert!

1 cup (20 g) fresh baby spinach

10 Medjool dates, pitted

2 ripe avocados

¼ cup (25 g) unsweetened cocoa powder

1 to 2 tablespoons pure maple syrup

1½ teaspoons espresso powder (optional)

1 teaspoon pure vanilla extract

Pinch of sea salt

4 to 6 mini chocolate candies, such as M&M's Minis (omit for children under the age of two)

① Chop the baby spinach in a food processor or high-powered blender.

② With a sharp knife, cut each date into four pieces and add them to the spinach in the processor. Pulse to create a paste.

③ Cut the avocado in half, remove the pit, and scoop the flesh into the food processor. Add the cocoa, 1 tablespoon of the maple syrup, the espresso powder (if using), vanilla, and salt and blend until smooth. Taste and stir in more syrup if desired.

④ Pour the mixture into 4 to 6 individual pudding cups that are at least 2 inches (5 cm) deep. Using a skewer or

a coffee stir stick, press one candy into the center of each pudding cup. That's the surprise!

5 Refrigerate until cold and firm, about 45 minutes.

All Kids Can . . .

- Cut and pit the avocados with a kid-safe knife

- Put the spinach in the processor (with an adult's help)
- Pulse the spinach to the desired consistency (with an adult's help)
- Add the other ingredients to the processor (with an adult's help)
- Use a skewer to press one candy into each pudding cup

Part Three

SUMMER VEGETABLES

Ah, summer! Colorful vegetables seem to be everywhere: farmer's markets, small roadside stands, bountiful neighborhood gardens, and overflowing bins at the grocery store. Now is the time to take advantage of all the opportunities for your child to interact with many different crops. Encourage him to explore, carrying his own canvas bag, picking out produce, and asking questions of the vendors. Embrace the teachable moments to discuss nutrition and all the new recipes you might create with his selections. Sample new produce whenever you can—and if it's an accomplishment for your child simply to carry the little paper cup that holds one solitary piece of cucumber, celebrate that task! Let him take it at his own pace and focus on the joy of being together.

BELL PEPPERS

What sweet vegetable comes in a rainbow of colors, such as red, yellow, orange, green, white, and purple? Bell peppers, of course! The longer the pepper stays on the plant, the sweeter it becomes, and according to *The Old Farmer's Almanac*,[1] the more mature peppers have more vitamin C, which boosts the body's immune system. Green peppers are the least sweet and more peppery in flavor because they are picked so early. Green peppers are just red peppers that are harvested before they have a chance to turn red and sweeten up!

EXPOSE

Pepper Pets

One of the delightful things about bell peppers is that they come in many shapes, sizes, and colors. This variety makes them ideal for creating a menagerie of pepper pets, and you'll be able to use the same peppers in upcoming recipes in this chapter.

What you'll need:

- 3 bell peppers for each person, of various shapes and colors
- Toothpicks
- Black olives
- Child-safe knives and scissors

- YouTube (a wonderful source for videos on how to make frogs, elephants, and other animals from vegetables, especially peppers; I'm a fan of letting kids come up with their own animal shapes—let them try out ideas with just a little guidance from you)

What to do:

PARENTS AND KIDS: Cut shapes, use toothpicks to attach pieces of pepper for legs, ears, or silly long noses, and add slices of olives for a camel's eyebrows, fringed eyelashes on a llama, or beady eyes for a snake. Consider slicing the pepper to create rings (terrific for forming elephant ears) or slicing off the top and cutting out eyes, a nose, and mouth to create a mini animal jack-o'-lantern.

How your child benefits

Many fine motor skills naturally come into play when doing crafts like cutting up peppers to make animal shapes, but this activity has a strong cognitive component, too. Kids must visualize an animal in their mind and then problem solve for ways to create the body parts, such as a head, neck, or hooves, out of the pieces of peppers and olives in front of them. How will we make all the parts stick together? How big should the head be, as compared to the body? Kids will do best if cued to stop, think, and plan which pieces to cut first. Should we save a big pepper for the elephant's body? Will we need long skinny peppers to create the trunk, or can we cut a piece from this big pepper instead? Visual learning, decision making, problem solving: This simple craft with peppers produces meaningful brain challenges for kids!

Pepper Shish Kebabs

TOTAL TIME: 45 minutes PREP: 20 minutes COOK: 15 to 25 minutes SERVES: 4 to 6

Let kids make these kebabs by trying to spear peppers on wood or metal skewers in the order of the colors of the rainbow: red, orange, yellow, green, blue, indigo, violet. Teach them this silly sentence to help them remember the sequence: "Ricky Offered You Gobs of Beautiful Inviting Vegetables."

3 or 4 medium bell peppers in various colors, seeded and cut into 1-inch (2.5 cm) pieces

Other vegetables or fruits for shades of blue, indigo, and violet, including seedless grapes, purple peppers, red onions, eggplant, red cabbage, or purple carrots, cut into 1-inch (2.5 cm) pieces

1 to 2 tablespoons extra virgin olive oil

Salt and black pepper to taste

❶ Soak wooden skewers for 15 minutes in water, or use metal skewers.

❷ Preheat the oven to 400°F (200°C).

❸ Toss the bell peppers and the other vegetables and fruits in a large bowl with the oil, salt, and black pepper.

❹ Pierce each piece of vegetable or fruit onto skewers in the order of the colors of the rainbow. Place the skewers on a baking sheet and roast for 15 to 25 minutes, until the vegetables are softened to your liking.

❺ Cool slightly before serving. If metal skewers are used, remove the veggies to serve them, so that little hands don't get burned.

- Wash, seed, and cut vegetables and fruits with a kid-safe knife
- Toss vegetables and fruits with oil, salt, and pepper
- Thread vegetables or fruits onto skewers (with an adult's help)
- Line up the kebabs on the baking sheet

Bell Pepper Baseballs

TOTAL TIME: 4½ to 8½ hours PREP: 30 minutes COOK: 4 to 8 hours
MAKES: 10 large meatballs

Each of the baseball-sized meatballs in this slow-cooker project has either yellow, red, or green peppers inside. Except one—it has all three colors! Who will get the lucky meatball? I include a high-quality sausage in this recipe to add to the depth of flavor. Like other processed meats, sausage is a "sometimes food" in my house, usually included in Italian dishes for a savory quality. If you'd prefer to omit processed meat altogether, just use twice as much hamburger for this dish and perhaps a pinch more of all the seasonings.

3 teaspoons extra virgin olive oil
½ medium green bell pepper, seeded and chopped into pea-sized chunks
½ medium red bell pepper, seeded and chopped into pea-sized chunks
½ medium yellow bell pepper, seeded and chopped into pea-sized chunks
½ medium onion, chopped into pea-sized chunks
3 teaspoons minced garlic
1 large egg
1 tablespoon dried oregano
2 teaspoons dried basil
¼ teaspoon salt
⅛ teaspoon black pepper
1 pound (455 g) lean ground beef
1 pound (455 g) ground Italian sausage
1 cup (100 g) grated Parmesan
1 cup (80 g) rolled oats (gluten-free if needed)
½ cup (50 g) dried bread crumbs (gluten-free if needed)
One 24-ounce (680 g) jar tomato-based pasta sauce (my favorite is any with basil, garlic, and onion, and no corn syrup)

❶ In a medium skillet, heat 1 teaspoon of the oil and sauté the green bell pepper and a third of the onion until softened. Stir in 1 teaspoon of the garlic and sauté for another minute. Transfer the veggies to a bowl. Repeat with the red bell pepper and then the yellow bell pepper.

❷ While the onions and peppers are cooling, whisk together the egg, oregano, basil, salt, and black pepper in a large bowl. Add the beef, sausage, and Parmesan, then add the oats and bread crumbs. Mix the ingredients together thoroughly with your hands, squishing the mixture between your fingers to combine well. (See page 113 for information about safe handling of raw meat.)

❸ Divide the meat mixture into three equal portions, transferring them to their own separate bowls. Add the bell pepper mixture from each skillet into each of the three bowls and mix with your hands to combine.

❹ For the lucky meatball, which has some bell peppers of each color, use a little bit of the mixture from each bowl to make a baseball-sized meatball by rolling the mixture together with your hands. Push in any obvious pieces so that only one color is visible. Then make three meatballs of a single bell pepper color with each mixture.

❺ Pour about a third of the tomato sauce into a large slow cooker and spread it evenly across the bottom.

6 Place all the meatballs in the slow cooker and pour the remaining tomato sauce over the top, coating well. Cook on high for 4 hours or on low for 8 hours. Meatballs can remain on "warm" in the slow cooker for up to 1½ hours before needing refrigeration.

All Kids Can . . .

- Wash, dry, and seed the peppers
- Chop the vegetables with a kid-safe knife, keeping different bell pepper colors separate
- Put the veggies in the skillet (with adult supervision)
- Whisk the egg mixture
- Pour the sauce and spread it onto the bottom of the slow cooker

- Place the meatballs in the slow cooker with tongs

Plus, Big Kids Can . . .

- Squish the meat mixture, using safe handling techniques on page 113
- Divide the meat mixture into thirds
- Form the meatballs

Rainbow Pizza

TOTAL TIME: 30 to 40 minutes **PREP:** 20 minutes **COOK:** 10 to 20 minutes
MAKES: 8 to 10 slices

Green, red, yellow, and orange bell peppers create four of the seven colors of the rainbow on this prismatic pizza. Red onions create the final hues of blue, indigo, and violet. I've included two simple options for the light coating of sauce that holds all the colors in place, one savory and one slightly sweet.

One large pizza crust (make your own from scratch, use frozen dough or a mix, or use a ready-made pizza crust; gluten-free if needed)

Olive oil for sautéing

½ medium green bell pepper, seeded and chopped into pea-sized chunks

½ medium orange bell pepper, seeded and chopped into pea-sized chunks

½ medium red bell pepper, seeded and chopped into pea-sized chunks

½ medium yellow bell pepper, seeded and chopped into pea-sized chunks

½ medium red onion, chopped into pea-sized chunks

Salt and black pepper to taste

1 cup (100 g) grated Parmesan

OPTION 1: SMOOTH CHEESE SAUCE

1½ cups (370 g) ricotta

½ cup (55 g) shredded mozzarella

1 tablespoon dried basil

1 tablespoon honey (optional)

½ teaspoon salt

OPTION 2: PESTO

1 cup (230 g) pesto (store-bought is fine)

1 to 2 tablespoons extra virgin olive oil, if needed

❶ Preheat the oven per the directions for the recipe, dough mix, or store-bought pizza crust.

❷ In a large skillet, heat the oil and sauté each color of bell pepper and the onion separately until softened, adding salt and black pepper to taste. As you go along, remove the cooked vegetables and place the different colors of bell peppers and the onion on separate doubled sheets of paper towels to cool slightly before assembling the pizza.

❸ To make the Smooth Cheese Sauce, mix all the ingredients together. To prepare the Pesto, add the oil if the pesto is too thick to spread on the pizza crust.

❹ Spread the Smooth Cheese Sauce or Pesto lightly over the pizza crust, avoiding the outer edge of the crust. Top the pizza by assembling the bell peppers in concentric circles of rainbow colors, starting with red in the center of the pizza and then building outward with orange, yellow, green, and blue (shades of purple).

❺ Bake the pizza per the recipe or package directions, until the edges of the crust are brown and the center is cooked through.

❻ Remove from the oven and top with the Parmesan. To serve, cut the pizza down the middle to create two rainbows or half circles. Cut the rainbows into individual (traditional) pizza pie slices. Serve each rainbow on a large plate for kids to pass and help themselves to a slice of the rainbow!

All Kids Can . . .

- Help prepare the pizza crust
- Wash, dry, and seed the peppers
- Chop the vegetables with a kid-safe knife, keeping them sorted by color
- Put the veggies in the skillet (with adult supervision)
- Spread sauce on the pizza crust
- Arrange the vegetables by color, according to the rainbow, on the pizza crust
- Top the pizza with the Parmesan
- Assemble cut slices of pizza on serving plates to form a rainbow

A Sweet Treat: Cherry-Red Pepper Ice Cream

TOTAL TIME: 30 minutes MAKES: 8 servings

Kids *love* this method of making ice cream! If you have an ice cream machine to make the recipe, this treat will be less labor-intensive, of course. But why not get a little exercise by shaking up some scrumptious homemade ice cream that includes a large red bell pepper in the mix?

1 large red bell pepper, washed, seeded, and cut into small chunks
1 cup (260 g) frozen cherries
1 cup (240 ml) 2 percent milk
1 cup (240 ml) heavy cream
½ cup (100 g) sugar
½ teaspoon pure vanilla extract
1 cup (290 g) plus a pinch salt
10 cups (1.4 kg) ice

❶ Blend the bell pepper, cherries, milk, cream, sugar, vanilla, and pinch of salt in a high-powered blender until only small flecks of pepper and cherry skin are apparent.

❷ Pour equal amounts of the mixture into four individual quart-sized plastic bags, sealing tightly and carefully squeezing out most of the air in the process. Place three of the four bags in the freezer to keep them very cold until you're ready for the next steps.

❸ Combine ¼ cup (75 g) salt and 2½ cups (350 g) ice in a gallon-sized plastic bag. Seal tightly and shake to mix.

❹ Unseal the gallon bag and insert the fourth bag of ice cream mixture into the bag of ice, sealing tightly again. Fold a thick hand towel around the bag (just in case it leaks and because it is *cold*!). Shake the bag for 10 minutes, turning it over occasionally to make sure it is mixing well. Once the ice cream is frozen, put this first batch in the freezer. Repeat the process with the other bags of ice cream mixture, replacing the ice and salt each time—or if you have lots of kids in the kitchen, make additional ice bags and get them all shaking at once!

5 When the mixture appears firm, simply cut off the corner of the bag and squeeze the ice cream into cones or bowls. Store the remaining ice cream in the same bag in the freezer, squeezing out extra air each time you serve some to ensure freshness.

All Kids Can . . .

- Wash, dry, and seed the bell pepper
- Chop the pepper into chunks with a kid-safe knife
- Add the ingredients to the blender

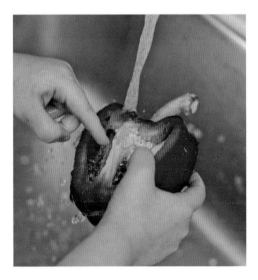

- Turn the blender on and off (with adult supervision)
- Help fill the quart-size bags with the ice cream mixture
- Help fill the gallon bag with ice and salt
- Shake the bags
- Squeeze the ice cream into bowls

TIP

Although you can put the bags of ice cream mix in the freezer without shaking them, the mixture will freeze into crystals and become hard with time. The effort of shaking mixes tiny air bubbles into the blend, giving the ice cream a smooth, creamier texture. The amount of fat in the mix also creates a smoother texture—premium ice creams have the highest percentage of milk fat, higher than this recipe. The smoothest, creamiest ice cream is made in machines that freeze the mixture while rapidly churning in the air bubbles. But the "shake the bag" method is a lot more fun! This is one time I suggest that you step out of the kitchen and into the backyard while the children are busy with a project. It's unlikely that the bags will unseal while shaking—but don't say I didn't warn you! Double-check those seals on each bag . . . just in case.

CORN

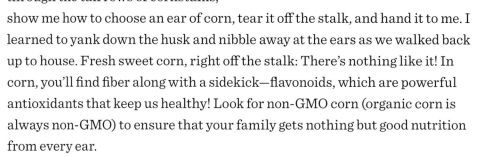

When I was a little girl, one of the first vegetables I learned to eat was raw corn, right out of our family's garden. My dad would walk me through the tall rows of cornstalks, show me how to choose an ear of corn, tear it off the stalk, and hand it to me. I learned to yank down the husk and nibble away at the ears as we walked back up to house. Fresh sweet corn, right off the stalk: There's nothing like it! In corn, you'll find fiber along with a sidekick—flavonoids, which are powerful antioxidants that keep us healthy! Look for non-GMO corn (organic corn is always non-GMO) to ensure that your family gets nothing but good nutrition from every ear.

EXPOSE

Corn-Husking Contest

The tactile experience of husking (sometimes called shucking) includes pulling away the leaves, the silky strings that lie beneath the leaves, and the tassel at the top of the ear. Be forewarned: There may be a tiny worm beneath that tassel! Some kids delight in finding a worm, and you might even have a special prize for anyone who finds one. But for those who aren't fond of wriggling friends in their food, just pull down the tassels before the game and quietly evict any little creatures.

What you'll need:

- 2 or 3 ears of corn per person (try to buy the freshest ears possible, since those will be sweetest raw)
- Timer

What to do:

PARENTS AND KIDS: Everyone grabs an ear of corn; the youngest person starts the timer and says "Go!" The first person with a clean ear of corn wins! For a more advanced version of this game, the winner must shuck the ear of corn and take a bite before stopping the timer. If anyone is hesitant about taking a bite of corn—just have fun, and the bite will come in its own time.

How your child benefits

Husking corn exposes kids to different kinds of textures, including the stiff leaves, the silky threads, and the kernels from the tip to the base of the ear. Kids who are hesitant to try new foods need exposure to various textures to experience food at the most basic level. When we introduce new foods in whole form, like an ear of corn, we are helping kids get to know it and make friends with it. Playing games such as this corn-husking race keeps any hesitation at bay while kids focus on the contest. Another plus is that the heavy pull required to remove the leaves is calming: When we compress our joints through heavy work, it helps quiet our bodies.

Corn Salsa

TOTAL TIME: 45 minutes (including 30 minutes in the fridge) MAKES: about 3 cups (780 g) salsa

Corn is the star of the show in this mild salsa. Gently stir in some chunks of heart-healthy avocado, pair it with corn tortilla chips for dipping, and see who can get the tallest scoop of salsa onto one chip! This salsa is extra flavorful if you refrigerate it for a half hour before eating, but it's hard to wait!

2 cups (360 g) drained canned corn kernels or fresh sweet corn

3 small plum tomatoes, seeded and chopped

½ small red onion, finely diced

¼ cup (5 g) finely chopped fresh cilantro (use parsley if your child is not a cilantro fan!)

1 cup (240 g) rinsed and drained canned black beans (optional)

¼ teaspoon salt, plus more to taste

2 to 3 tablespoons extra virgin olive oil (see Parenting in the Kitchen)

2 to 3 tablespoons fresh lime juice

Black pepper to taste

1 to 2 large avocados, pitted, peeled, and diced

❶ In a large bowl, combine the corn, tomatoes, onion, cilantro, beans (if using), and ¼ teaspoon salt.

❷ In a small bowl, whisk together the olive oil and lime juice, adding more or less of either to suit your taste buds. Season with pepper and more salt, if desired.

❸ Stir the corn mixture and the dressing together. Cover and refrigerate for 30 minutes.

❹ When you're ready to dig in, gently stir in the avocado chunks and serve.

- Wash and dry the tomatoes and avocados
- Rinse and drain the beans (if using)
- Juice the limes
- Seed and chop the tomatoes using a kid-safe knife

- Combine the corn mixture ingredients in a bowl
- Whisk together the oil and lime juice
- Mix the dressing with the corn mixture
- Stir in the avocado
- Add salt and pepper to taste

PARENTING IN THE KITCHEN

Throughout the recipes in this book, you'll notice that I encourage you and your kids to taste, taste, and taste again. This recipe is the perfect example of why it's important to master the art of taste testing. Everyone seems to have a slightly different preference when it comes to dressings. Some like their dressing to be a bit acidic (more lime) and others prefer that the smoothness of the oil dominates the flavors. Some kids are still learning about tomatoes, beans, or avocados, and they may prefer more or less of these ingredients in this recipe. Play with the combination. This recipe has a touch of salt, but depending on the ingredients you choose, it may need a touch more. Taste as you go. Ask your kids, "What do you think? Does it need more of something?" Not only will you help develop your child's palate, but he'll also gain confidence in his ability to taste almost anything and to change any dish to suit his liking.

Corny Corn Bread with Honey Butter

TOTAL TIME: 35 minutes PREP: 15 minutes COOK: 20 minutes MAKES: 12 pieces

Corn bread is meant to have a crunchier texture than typical breads, but that grittiness can be a bit much for kids who may be more used to spongy, soft sandwich bread. For this recipe, I soak the cornmeal in the buttermilk before mixing up the batter. This step softens the cornmeal, taking away that coarse texture but leaving the lovely flavor of sweet corn to complement the honey butter melted on top. For extra moist bread, soak the cornmeal for up to 2 hours on the kitchen counter, making sure to use fresh cultured buttermilk.

1 cup (240 ml) buttermilk

1 cup (130 g) fine stone-ground cornmeal (gluten-free if needed)

¼ cup (60 ml) plus 1 tablespoon melted coconut oil (cooled slightly)

½ cup (65 g) all-purpose flour (gluten-free if needed)

½ cup (65 g) cornstarch

¼ cup (50 g) sugar

1 tablespoon baking powder (gluten-free if needed)

½ teaspoon salt

2 medium eggs, beaten

1½ cups (270 g) frozen corn kernels, thawed

HONEY BUTTER

½ cup (115 g) salted butter, at room temperature

2 tablespoon honey, plus more if desired

❶ In a large bowl, stir together the buttermilk and cornmeal. Let the mixture sit for 15 minutes.

❷ Prepare an 8 × 8-inch (20 × 20 cm) baking dish by coating the sides and bottom with 1 tablespoon of the coconut oil. Turn the oven on to 400°F (200°C) and place the empty greased dish in the oven to heat.

❸ In a medium bowl, whisk together the flour, cornstarch, sugar, baking powder, and salt.

4 Stir the remaining ¼ cup (60 ml) coconut oil and the eggs into the cornmeal mixture.

5 Add the flour mixture to the cornmeal mixture. Stir in the corn kernels.

6 Take the hot pan out of the oven. Pour the batter into the pan and immediately return it to the oven to bake for 20 minutes, or until the sides are browned. (Preheating the pan ensures crispiness on the sides and bottom of the bread.)

7 To make the Honey Butter, combine the butter with the honey, using a hand mixer. Add more honey if desired.

8 Serve the bread warm with the Honey Butter.

All Kids Can . . .

- Pour the buttermilk from the carton into a measuring cup
- Stir and soak the cornmeal
- Coat the pan with coconut oil
- Whisk the dry ingredients
- Stir the oil and eggs into the cornmeal mixture
- Add the dry mixture to the cornmeal mixture
- Stir in the corn kernels
- Make the Honey Butter (with adult supervision if using an electric mixer)

Corn Chowder

TOTAL TIME: 1 hour PREP: 25 minutes COOK: 25 to 30 minutes SERVES: 6 with leftovers

Just because it's summer, the warm weather shouldn't stop you from enjoying a lovely bowl of chowder at the end of the day. This recipe is so quick, I recommend making it the day before and refrigerating overnight, for optimal flavor. But if you decide to whip it up just before an evening supper on the front porch, that's great, too!

5 strips thick-cut bacon

4 large potatoes, peeled and cut into 1-inch (2.5 cm) chunks

1 medium onion, finely chopped

2 tablespoons all-purpose flour (gluten-free if needed)

3 cups (720 ml) chicken or vegetable broth

1½ cups (270 g) frozen, canned (drained), or fresh sweet corn, plus a few tablespoons for garnish

2 tablespoons dried parsley

2 teaspoons dried summer savory

1½ teaspoons salt, plus more to taste

½ teaspoon garlic powder

1 bay leaf

4 cups (960 ml) milk (use the fat content of your choice; I prefer 2 percent)

Black pepper to taste

2 tablespoons chopped fresh chives (optional)

❶ In a large, heavy pot, brown the bacon over medium-high heat until it's just slightly crispy, then remove it from the pan and place it on paper towels to drain.

❷ Carefully pour off most of the bacon drippings from the pot, leaving about 2 tablespoons for sautéing the potatoes and onion.

❸ Add the potatoes and onion to the pot, cooking to soften slightly for 5 minutes. Slowly stir in the flour and continue stirring for 2 minutes.

4 Add the broth, corn, parsley, savory, salt, garlic powder, and bay leaf to the pot and bring the soup to a boil. Immediately reduce the heat to medium-low. Cover the pot and simmer until the potatoes are tender, 15 to 20 minutes.

5 Before adding the milk, temper it by pouring it into a large bowl and gradually stirring in small amounts of the hot broth to warm it. Then, add the milk and broth combination to the pot.

6 Warm the soup over low heat to your desired serving temperature. Crumble most of the bacon into the pot, eating at least three crumbles in the process (no one will know). Season with more salt, if needed, and pepper.

7 Remove the bay leaf. Serve with a sprinkling of sweet corn kernels, chopped chives (if using), and the remaining bacon crumbles on top.

All Kids Can . . .

- Wash the potatoes
- Chop the potatoes and chives with a kid-safe knife
- Help measure all ingredients
- Add ingredients to the pot (with an adult's help)
- Crumble the bacon
- Add salt and pepper to taste, blowing on small samples of the soup before tasting

Plus, Big Kids Can . . .

- Peel the potatoes (with adult supervision)
- Brown the bacon (with adult supervision)
- Chop the onions (with adult supervision)
- Sauté the potatoes and onion and add the additional ingredients

A Sweet Treat: Corny Glazed Mini Doughnuts

TOTAL TIME: 25 to 30 minutes PREP: 15 minutes COOK: 10 to 12 minutes
MAKES: 24 mini doughnuts

Kids love anything in miniature, especially doughnuts. These doughnuts bake with a glaze built right in! This recipe will require two mini-doughnut pans (with twelve cavities each).

Nonstick cooking spray
⅔ cup (85 g) fine stone-ground yellow cornmeal (gluten-free if needed)
⅓ cup (40 g) all-purpose flour (gluten-free if needed)
¾ teaspoon baking powder (gluten-free if needed)
¾ teaspoon baking soda
Pinch of salt
One 6-ounce (170 g) container blueberry low-fat yogurt (mixed in, not fruit on the bottom)
¼ cup (40 g) drained canned sweet corn
¼ cup (50 g) plus 2 tablespoons sugar
1 large egg, beaten
1 tablespoon canola oil
2 teaspoons lemon juice

❶ Preheat the oven to 400°F (200°C). Spray the cavities and surface of two mini-doughnut pans with nonstick cooking spray.

❷ In a large bowl, whisk together the cornmeal, flour, baking powder, baking soda, and salt.

❸ In a medium bowl, stir together the yogurt, corn, ¼ cup (50 g) of the sugar, egg, oil, and lemon juice.

❹ Add the yogurt mixture to the cornmeal mixture, folding carefully to mix. (Do not overmix.)

5 Using a measuring spoon, scoop 1 tablespoon of the dough and form it into a ball. Press the ball into one of the cavities of the doughnut pan, until the center post of the cavity pokes through the dough. Gently flatten the top of the dough so that it takes on the shape of a doughnut. Repeat with the rest of the dough.

6 Sprinkle the remaining 2 tablespoons sugar over the tops of the doughnuts.

7 Bake for 10 to 12 minutes, until a toothpick inserted into a doughnut comes out clean.

8 Remove the pans from the oven and let them cool for 2 minutes before flipping them over to deposit the doughnuts on a cooling rack. Caution: The sugar-glaze topping will be hot!

9 Allow the doughnuts to cool a bit before serving.

All Kids Can . . .

- Prep the doughnut pan
- Whisk the dry ingredients
- Mix the wet ingredients together
- Fold the wet and dry ingredients together
- Create balls of dough and press them into the pans
- Sprinkle the sugar on top

CUCUMBERS

The flavinols in cucumbers have a very cool superpower—they keep us hydrated and help reduce inflammation. To ensure that your cucumbers are fresh and rich in flavinols, choose firm "cukes" that are medium to dark green. Avoid any that have wrinkled tips! Store cucumbers in the refrigerator in the produce drawer so that they're protected from light and get minimal exposure to air to prevent spoilage.

EXPOSE
Cucumber Caterpillars

One of my favorite books to read to young kids in feeding therapy is Eric Carle's *The Very Hungry Caterpillar*. It always leads to building green caterpillars with little red heads, just like the one in the book. Choose the foods you love and pair them with cucumber slices to make your own very hungry caterpillar! The trick is to pair a child's preferred vegetable or fruit with one the child is exploring for the first time. So, if your child loves green apples, alternate green apple slices with the cucumbers. Combining a little bit of a preferred food with a few slices of a "learning food" can bridge the gap between avoidance and acceptance.

What you'll need:

- White paper
- Colored pencils or crayons
- ½ English cucumber per person, sliced, for the caterpillar's body (An English cucumber is longer and skinnier than a traditional cucumber, with almost no seeds in the center. The skin is thinner and easier to bite into, making it inviting for hesitant eaters to take that very first crunch!)
- Other fruits and veggies cut into circles (for the caterpillar's body), such as green apples, kiwi, jicama, zucchini, or honeydew melon
- ½ cherry tomato per person
- Extra pieces of vegetables you have on hand, such as spinach leaves, pea pods or corn kernels—whatever is in your refrigerator!

What to do:

PARENTS AND KIDS:
Create your own caterpillars on white paper by overlapping cucumber slices and favorite green fruits and vegetables. Add half of a tomato for the head, then draw in the antennae and feet, or add grass and trees to the background. Draw some favorite foods that you'd love to eat if you could eat right through them, just like the very hungry caterpillar did!

How your child benefits

This activity focuses on pattern recognition, both visually and through language. Your child is learning to see the many parts that make up a whole. She is drawing in the legs and the antennae to complete the bigger picture in her mind of the very hungry caterpillar. Learning to create and recognize patterns is a crucial part of mathematical learning, plus it's a vital component of language use, memory, and comprehension. Support the development of these skills by showing the child the unique pattern you created on your paper, and see if she can tell you what it is. A pattern could be an arrangement of colors or shapes, a series of nouns like "zucchini, cucumber, zucchini, zucchini, cucumber," or categories such as "vegetable, fruit, vegetable, vegetable, fruit."

EXPLORE
Cucumber Spirals

TOTAL TIME: 15 to 25 minutes SERVES: 6 to 8

Part of the satisfaction of preparing this salad can be the mesmerizing activity of watching spirals of cucumbers and other vegetables twirl into a bowl straight from the machine. But if you don't own a spiralizer, no worries! Many stores have spiralized vegetables packaged and ready to take home, or you can improvise on the preparation by slicing vegetables julienne-style.

1 tablespoon plus 1 teaspoon apple cider vinegar
1 tablespoon extra virgin olive oil
1 tablespoon honey
⅛ teaspoon salt
Pinch of black pepper (optional)
2 Granny Smith apples, sliced for spiralizing or julienned
Lemon juice for the apples
2 English cucumbers
1 large jicama, prepared for spiralizing or julienned
1 large carrot, prepared for spiralizing or julienned (optional)
1 scallion, thinly sliced (optional)

❶ In a small bowl, whisk together the vinegar, oil, honey, salt, and pepper (if using).

❷ Spiralize the apples over a large bowl and toss with the lemon juice.

❸ Spiralize the cucumbers, jicama, and carrot (if using) over the bowl of spiralized apple. Using kitchen shears, cut the spirals into slightly shorter pieces before they fall into the bowl to make them easier to toss in the dressing.

❹ Toss with the dressing and scallions (if desired) and serve.

All Kids Can . . .

- Wash and dry the apples, cucumbers, jicama, carrot, and scallions
- Peel the jicama with a kid-safe knife (and an adult's help)
- Help spiralize the apples, cucumbers, jicama, and carrot
- Whisk the dressing

- Toss all the ingredients together
- Sprinkle the scallions before serving (if using)

Plus, Big Kids Can . . .

- Peel the jicama and carrot (with adult supervision)

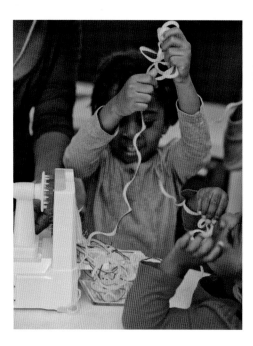

Filled Cucumber Cups

TOTAL TIME: 30 minutes PREP: 15 minutes SERVES: 6

Grab a melon baller and scoop out the center from a piece of cucumber, fill with your favorite dip from the combinations below, and you've got a finger food that makes an appealing appetizer, a handy after-school snack, or a healthy lunch-box treat! See Parenting in the Kitchen to modify this recipe for toddlers.

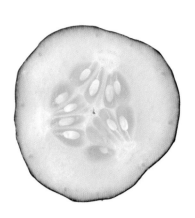

2 English cucumbers (other varieties will work, but these have minimal to no seeds)

FILLING OPTION 1: PESTO GOAT CHEESE

4 ounces (115 g) soft goat cheese
2 to 3 tablespoons pesto (store-bought is fine)
2 tablespoons pine nuts (optional)
2 leaves fresh basil, julienned (optional)
Cherry tomatoes, halved (optional)

FILLING OPTION 2: DILL AND BACON CREAM CHEESE

¼ cup (55 g) cream cheese
¼ cup (55 g) plain 2 percent Greek yogurt
1 strip cooked bacon, crumbled into tiny pieces, plus 1 more strip cooked and crumbled for garnish (optional)
1 teaspoon celery salt
1 teaspoon dried dill
1 teaspoon onion flakes
1 sprig fresh dill (optional)

FILLING OPTION 3: TUNA SALAD

One 5-ounce (142 g) can white albacore tuna packed in water, drained well
¼ cup (60 g) mayonnaise, or slightly more to taste
1 to 2 tablespoons pickle relish
Pinch of black pepper
3 tablespoons shredded cheddar (optional)
1 sprig fresh dill (optional)

❶ Use a vegetable peeler to remove four strips of peel down the length of each cucumber, leaving four dark green strips unpeeled. Cut off the ends of each cucumber and cut the remainder into ¾-inch (2 cm) rounds.

2 Using a small melon baller, scoop out the seeds or the center of each round, being careful not to poke through the bottom.

3 To make Filling Option 1, blend the goat cheese and pesto until evenly mixed. Use the melon baller to place filling in each cup. Garnish each, if desired, with pine nuts, a sliver of julienned basil, or a cherry tomato half.

4 To make Filling Option 2, blend the cream cheese, yogurt, bacon, and spices until evenly mixed. Use the melon baller to place filling in each cup. Garnish each, if desired, with more bacon crumbles, fresh dill, or both.

5 To make Filling Option 3, blend the tuna, mayonnaise, relish, and pepper until evenly mixed. Use the melon baller to place filling in each cup. Garnish each, if desired, with shredded cheddar or fresh dill. (This recipe may have enough tuna left over for a sandwich!)

6 Arrange the cucumber cups on a platter and serve.

All Kids Can . . .

- Wash and dry the cucumbers
- Cut the cucumbers into rounds with a kid-safe knife

- Use a melon baller to scoop out the centers of the cucumber pieces (with an adult's help)
- Chop or cut the basil and dill garnishes with a kid-safe knife or shears
- Mix the fillings
- Fill the cucumber cups and arrange them on a platter
- Add garnishes

Plus, Big Kids Can . . .

- Peel the cucumbers (with adult supervision)

PARENTING IN THE KITCHEN

If you have toddlers in your family, consider using these spreads for cucumber "sandwiches," to ensure that they don't put a whole chunk of cucumber in their mouths: Slice the cucumbers thinly, spread a tiny bit of dip on one cucumber slice, then top it with another slice. Another option would be to offer all three spreads as dips and cut the cucumbers into dipping sticks, about the width of a small child's finger.

Quinoa Cucumber Salad

TOTAL TIME: 30 minutes, not including quinoa cooking time or 1 hour in fridge PREP: 20 minutes
SERVES: 4

The texture of quinoa can feel a little too crumbly for some kids. The trick to serving this protein-packed grain is to pair it with the right dressing and mix it with vegetables that have plenty of moisture, like tomatoes and cucumbers.

1 cup (170 g) quinoa, cooked per package directions
1 English cucumber (or other variety, with the pulpy center removed), seeded and chopped
2 plum tomatoes, seeded and finely chopped
1 cup (45 g) finely chopped fresh flat-leaf parsley
¼ cup (5 g) finely chopped fresh mint
¼ cup (20 g) finely sliced scallion
¼ cup (60 ml) fresh lemon juice
3 tablespoons extra virgin olive oil
1 small garlic clove, minced (optional)
Salt and black pepper to taste

❶ Mix the quinoa, cucumber, tomatoes, parsley, mint, and scallion in a large bowl.

❷ In a small bowl, whisk together the lemon juice, oil, and garlic (if using). Season with salt and pepper.

❸ Stir the dressing into the quinoa mixture, cover, and refrigerate for 1 hour, if possible, to allow the flavors to blend. If you'd like to serve it immediately, save some for the next day and you'll taste the difference!

All Kids Can . . .

- Help prepare the quinoa (with adult supervision)
- Wash and dry the cucumber, tomato, and herbs
- Seed and chop the cucumber with a kid-safe knife
- Tear or chop the herbs with a kid-safe knife
- Whisk the dressing
- Mix all the ingredients and season to taste

A Sweet Treat: Kids' Cucumber Cooler

TOTAL TIME: 20 minutes PREP: 15 minutes MAKES: 4 drinks

Half the fun of making this drink is the muddling! "Muddling" just means putting ingredients into a heavy glass or stone container (we'll use mason jars for this recipe) and then using a blunt tool to massage the ingredients in the bottom of the jar. This technique helps release all the different flavors so they can bind together, and it's a popular method for making summer drinks when fresh herbs and fruits are abundant. See Parenting in the Kitchen if you want to muddle more than just the dill.

4 small cucumbers, peeled and cut into small chunks, plus 4 thin slices for garnish
1 teaspoon finely chopped fresh dill
4 tablespoons agave syrup
4 tablespoons fresh lemon juice (about 2 lemons)
4 tablespoons fresh lime juice (about 2 limes)
1 cup (240 ml) club soda
Ice

❶ Blend the cucumber chunks in a high-powered blender until a thin puree has formed.

❷ Line up four mason jars and into each jar put a pinch of the dill and 1 tablespoon each of the agave syrup, lemon juice, and lime juice.

❸ Using a muddling tool (such as the back of a thick wooden spoon), gently push on the dill to blend the flavors. Don't muddle too hard! Too much force brings out the bitter oils in some herbs and fruits.

❹ Holding a small fine-mesh strainer over each jar, pour in the cucumber juice, dividing equally among the four jars. Discard the pulp.

❺ Top each jar with ¼ cup (60 ml) club soda and add ice.

6 Garnish each jar with a cucumber slice and serve with a straw, if desired.

All Kids Can . . .

- Wash and dry the cucumbers, dill, limes, and lemons
- Cut the cucumbers into chunks and cut slices for garnish
- Chop the dill
- Count tablespoons of juice
- Muddle the ingredients
- Add the club soda and garnish

Plus, Big Kids Can . . .

- Peel the cucumbers (with adult supervision)

PARENTING IN THE KITCHEN

Instead of measuring out a tablespoon of each juice, another option is to give your kids a peeled lemon and a peeled lime segment to muddle in the jar along with the agave and dill. Cucumbers can be muddled, too! Kids may want to adjust the flavor by squeezing a bit more agave or juice into their cooler. Let them make the decision about what improvements their drink needs to make it delish!

GREEN BEANS

There is a reason Jack could climb that beanstalk: The iron in green beans gave him a healthy heart for stamina, and the magnesium gave him strong bones to fight that giant! When I was a little girl, I would sit on the back porch and "snap" fresh green beans with my grandmother to break off the pointy tip of each bean before cooking. Today, I bring Kuhn Rikon Duck Snippers to feeding therapy sessions to snip off the ends of green beans when cooking with kids. They are shaped like a silly duck face and have rounded-off, child-friendly blades (just like the duck's bill) that are just sharp enough for this task, but not sharp enough to hurt little fingers. Sometimes I even let the kids use them, too!

EXPOSE
Tic-Tac-Toe

When kids make this tic-tac-toe game board with fresh green beans, they don't need to limit themselves to the traditional nine squares. How many green beans can they line up end to end to create a Connect Four–type game board that has at least forty squares? For more exposure to the veggies used in this book, try making the game pieces out of parsnip and carrot rounds or even using FunBites food cutters (see page 259). You'll need five of each piece if playing on a smaller board and twenty of each if you opt for making the larger board.

What you'll need:

- Fresh green beans
- A large, flat playing surface, like the kitchen table
- Two different colors of vegetables sliced into game pieces

What to do:

1 YOUNG KIDS: Make the traditional, smaller game board, using the green beans to create a three-by-three grid (like a hashtag) and slices of different-colored veggies (cucumber and carrots, for instance) to try to get three in a row.

2 OLDER KIDS: Create larger boards with more green beans, where the object is to get four in a row (up, down, or at a diagonal).

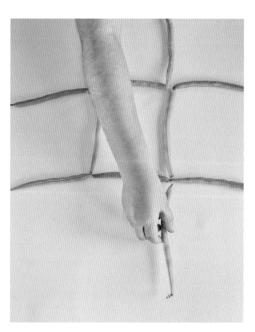

How your child benefits

The age-old game of tic-tac-toe teaches a child to predict next steps, a major component of problem solving and learning about strategy. They must observe what move their opponent made and consider what move their opponent might make next. This process becomes more complicated when using larger boards with more opportunities for placement of each playing piece. Kids begin to think ahead, planning out blocking strategies and ways to tempt the other player into making the wrong move. Meanwhile, kids are holding a variety of vegetables, studying the game board, maybe even pressing a veggie up to their lips as they concentrate on their next move. If they eat the game pieces while contemplating their winning strategy, that's OK, too.

Crispy Baked Green Beans and Dip

TOTAL TIME: 30 minutes PREP: 15 minutes COOK: 15 minutes SERVES: 6

Years ago, I would occasionally splurge on an order of deep-fried green beans accompanied by an onion-and-mayonnaise dip at a local restaurant in my hometown . . . until I made this simple recipe. Now, I indulge in this healthier version as often as I like without the guilt! With only five ingredients, this snack is simple to make—and the nutritious dip is a high-protein bowl of Greek yogurt with added seasoning!

Nonstick cooking spray

½ cup (50 g) dried bread crumbs (gluten-free if needed)

2 tablespoons packaged dill, ranch, or onion dip mix

1 pound (455 g) fresh green beans, washed, dried, and trimmed

2 large eggs, beaten

½ cup (115 g) plain 2 percent Greek yogurt

❶ Preheat the oven to 425°F (218°C). Line two baking sheets with foil and lightly coat the foil with cooking spray.

❷ Mix the bread crumbs and 1 tablespoon of the dip mix in a shallow bowl.

❸ Line up the green beans, beaten eggs, bread crumb mixture, and baking sheet in front of you.

❹ With one hand, dip a green bean into the beaten eggs and shake off any excess over the egg bowl before transferring the bean to the bread crumb mixture.

❺ With your other hand (the dry hand), coat the bean with the bread crumbs and place it on a baking sheet.

❻ Continue this process until all the beans are in a single layer on the baking sheets, then place the sheets in the oven for 10 minutes.

7 Combine the yogurt with the remaining tablespoon of dip mix.

8 Remove the baking sheets from the oven and turn the oven to broil. Turn each bean over and return the pans to the oven, allowing the exposed side of the beans to crisp under the broiler for 1 or 2 minutes. The bread crumbs will be slightly browned on the edges.

9 Remove the pans from the broiler and let the beans cool slightly before serving. Serve with the yogurt dip.

All Kids Can . . .

- Wash and dry the green beans
- Trim the ends of the green beans with kids' safety shears (see page 259)
- Line the baking sheets with foil
- Coat the foil with spray
- Beat the eggs with a fork
- Combine the ingredients for the dip

Plus, Big Kids Can . . .

- Dip the beans into the egg mixture and coat them with bread crumbs
- Use tongs to turn the beans over before broiling the bottoms (with adult supervision)

Pickled Green Beans

TOTAL TIME: 24 to 48 hours in the fridge PREP: 15 minutes
MAKES: 2 pint-sized (500 ml) jars of pickles

Refrigerator green bean pickles—no canning necessary! Have you ever noticed how much kids love pickles, especially the extra crunchy ones? When your kids crunch into one of these, they'll find the combination of tart and sweet irresistible. You'll need two pint-sized (500 ml) canning jars with lids for the recipe, so that you have one jar open and another waiting in the fridge when they ask for more the next day!

8 ounces (225 g) green beans
4 to 6 sprigs fresh dill
2 large garlic cloves, sliced
1 teaspoon mustard seeds
2 cups (480 ml) distilled white vinegar
2 cups (480 ml) bottled water or purified water (see Tip)
1 tablespoon plus 2 teaspoons sea salt
1 tablespoon plus 1 teaspoon sugar

❶ Wash and blanch the green beans in boiling water (see blanching instructions on page 81).

❷ Put half of the dill, garlic, and mustard seeds in each jar.

❸ Hold a stack of green beans in your fist up against the outside of a jar to see how they will stand up inside. Using kitchen shears, snip off any ends of the beans that reach past the top of the jar. Now, flip the beans over and snip off another half inch. Discard the ends. Do this with the rest of the beans.

❹ Put half of the beans in each jar, being careful not to pack them in too tightly. If you have a few beans left over, that's OK! Sprinkle a little salt over the leftovers and have a snack while you're pickling.

5 In a large saucepan, combine the vinegar, water, salt, and sugar. Bring this brine to a boil over high heat and boil for 2 minutes, stirring until the salt and sugar are dissolved. Remove the saucepan from the heat.

6 Carefully pour the brine into each jar, stopping ½ inch (13 mm) from the rim of the jar. The beans should be fully immersed in the liquid. Place the lids on the jars and refrigerate for 24 for 48 hours before serving.

7 Green bean pickles can be kept in the refrigerator for up to 4 weeks.

All Kids Can . . .

- Wash the green beans and the fresh dill
- Trim the ends of the green beans with kids' safety shears (see page 259)
- Divide ingredients into each jar

Plus, Big Kids Can . . .

- Boil the brine and pour it into the jars (with adult supervision)

TIP

When making pickles, the quality of the water used in the brine is almost as important as the vegetable itself. Hard water (lots of minerals in the water) make pickles taste, well, minerally. Consider using bottled water and a good-quality fine sea salt—not iodized salt, unless you want pickles that taste like iodine. As the beans soak in the brine, a chemical process known as osmosis occurs. In simple terms, *osmosis* means fluids passing in opposite directions across a membrane to achieve equilibrium. The brine and the water inside the bean trade places by passing through the skin of the bean, so that the water balance of the bean changes. The change in taste is created through a chemical process known as diffusion, where the flavors we added to the brine (salt, dill, garlic, and so on) have moved through the membrane of the plant cells and changed the taste and texture of the beans soaking in the brine. The result? Yummy pickles.

Veggie Stir-Fry

TOTAL TIME: 35 to 45 minutes PREP: 20 to 30 minutes COOK: 15 minutes SERVES: 4 to 6

This recipe comes from one of my favorite authors and childhood nutrition experts, Jill Castle (jillcastle.com). Jill and I collaborate on various projects together, and she always has practical tips to offer parents. Although you can use veggies fresh from the garden for Jill's veggie stir-fry, the amounts for some ingredients that would need prep work are set up so that you can easily make this colorful dish from time-saving packaged veggies from the store.

4 tablespoons canola oil

4 tablespoons soy sauce

1 medium onion, chopped

3 garlic cloves, minced

2 teaspoons minced ginger

One 10- or 12-ounce (283 or 340 g) package green beans (washed and ready to cook)

One 10- or 12-ounce (283 or 340 g) package julienned carrots (washed and ready to eat)

1 medium yellow bell pepper, cut into slices (see Tip)

1 to 2 pounds (455 to 905 g) peeled and deveined large raw shrimp (optional)

5 cups (975 g) cooked brown rice

❶ In a wok or large pan with deep sides, heat 2 tablespoons of the canola oil and 2 tablespoons of the soy sauce together over medium-high heat. Add the onion and sauté until soft. As each ingredient is added, stir occasionally to ensure even cooking (see Tip).

❷ Add the garlic and ginger and sauté for 1 minute. Add the remaining 2 tablespoons oil and 2 tablespoons soy sauce to the pan. Add the green beans, carrots, and bell pepper and cook for 5 to 8 minutes, until the veggies begin to soften (cook for a shorter time if you want crunchier vegetables).

❸ Add the shrimp (if using) and sauté everything together until the shrimp is cooked through (it will appear pink).

4 Serve with the rice. (See Parenting in the Kitchen for serving hesitant eaters.)

(See Parenting in the Kitchen for serving hesitant eaters.)

All Kids Can . . .

- Open the packages of beans and carrots (if using)
- Wash and dry the bell pepper
- Cut the bell pepper into slices with a kid-safe knife
- Hand parents or older kids cups of various ingredients for adding to the wok

Plus, Big Kids Can . . .

- Stir-fry the ingredients (with adult supervision)

TIP

The secret to stir-frying is to cut the ingredients into similar sizes and stir frequently. This ensures that all the surfaces of the food reach the heat on the sides of the wok and provides consistent taste and texture throughout the dish.

PARENTING IN THE KITCHEN

Before serving stir-fry over rice, consider deconstructing it for hesitant eaters. Using tongs, separate out a few beans and pieces of onion, carrot, and pepper. Include a few pieces of each on your child's plate, along with just a tiny bit of the mixed stir-fry over rice or noodles. Place a tablespoon of plain rice or noodles on the plate, too. Kids will often start by reaching for their favorite pieces and eventually try the mixed version. Remember, keep it underwhelming with just small samples to get started.

A Sweet Treat: Green Bean Bacon Bundles

TOTAL TIME: 45 to 50 minutes PREP: 10 minutes COOK: 35 to 40 minutes SERVES: 8

These bundles of green beans coated in brown sugar and wrapped in bacon are oh-so-good. I make just a few at a time, because they are extra sweet and bacon is a "sometimes" treat. They're also a little sticky, like eating cotton candy!

8 ounces (225 g) thick-cut bacon
3 ounces (85 g) green beans, washed, dried, and trimmed
½ cup (90 g) lightly packed light brown sugar

❶ Preheat the oven to 400°F (200°C). Line a rimmed baking sheet with foil for easy cleanup. Place a wire rack (a cooling rack for baking works nicely) on top of the foil.

❷ Divide the green beans into bundles of four to six beans, or create enough bundles for each strip of bacon.

❸ Put the sugar in a large bowl and dip both sides of a slice of bacon in the sugar to coat. Wrap the slice of bacon around a bundle of beans from end to end, like a corkscrew, and place the bundle on the wire rack. Continue with the remaining bacon slices and beans, leaving space between each bundle on the rack.

❹ Sprinkle the bundles with the remaining brown sugar. Bake for 20 minutes. Remove the pan from the oven and carefully flip over each bundle. Return the pan to the oven and bake for 15 to 20 more minutes, until crispy. These will be very hot due to the sugar coating. Be careful!

5 When the bundles are cool to the touch, serve them in short juice glasses, small mason jars, or some other narrow glass.

All Kids Can . . .

- Line the baking sheet with foil
- Wash and dry the green beans
- Count the bacon slices for each bundle
- Divide the green beans into bundles
- Sprinkle the assembled bundles with brown sugar

Plus, Big Kids Can . . .

- Coat the bacon with brown sugar
- Wrap the bacon around the bundles
- Place the assembled bundles on the wire rack

TOMATOES

Tomatoes are famous for having loads of lycopene, an antioxidant that helps fight diseases. To help your body use that lycopene, eat tomatoes with some healthy oils, such as olive oil. The beauty of a tomato is in the number of varieties! There are thousands of types worldwide, but most people tend to think in terms of size when doing their shopping, reaching for cherry versus globe tomatoes. Take a minute next time you're in the produce aisle to see how many different kinds you can find with your kids. The farmer's market is sure to have even more varieties, and harvest times peak at different times of the season, depending on the local climate. Make a habit of going to the farmer's market at least twice a month. You'll be amazed at the new offerings that show up every few weeks.

EXPOSE

Tomato Squirting Contest

Kids are often hesitant to bite into a tomato because the seeds and pulp squirt into their mouth. Show them the fun in the squirt by having a contest to see who can squirt the farthest!

What you'll need:

- 5 cherry tomatoes per person
- 2 or 3 sheets of white paper, taped end to end on the short side, per person
- Measuring stick
- Cloth or paper napkins (optional)

What to do:

1 PARENTS: Have each player sit at the table with the long paper sticking out in front of them; the short side should be aligned with the table's edge, beneath the player's chin. You can tie a napkin around each player's neck to protect clothing, if you want, but I like kids to get messy, so I always skip that part!

2 PARENTS AND KIDS: Each player picks up a tomato, bites into it one time, and measures how far she squirted it onto the paper. Whoever squirts the farthest, wins!

How your child benefits

With this activity, kids who shy away from tomatoes can get used to the squirt before ever taking a bite. But it's likely some of the tomatoes will end up being eaten in this game! Math skills (using a ruler) and cognitive problem-solving skills (What makes it squirt farther? Is it the force of the bite or the size of the tomato?) are part of the fun, too.

Tomato Toothpicks and Eight Different Dips

TOTAL TIME: 10 to 20 minutes SERVES: 4 to 6

One of the easiest ways to help kids adjust to the texture of a tomato is to pair it with a dip. While any toothpick will do for this recipe, your child will be more tempted to spear a tomato (which will already be sitting in a bit of dip) if you offer party picks with fringed tops or even decorative cupcake toppers. When you put the tomatoes in an ice cube tray, the sides of each cube hold them in place for easy spearing. Make as many as eight different dips for sampling!

ANY OF THE FOLLOWING DIPS (EACH IS ENOUGH TO FILL ONE SECTION OF AN ICE CUBE TRAY):

1 tablespoon sour cream + pinch of grated Parmesan + ⅛ teaspoon Dijon mustard

1 tablespoon hummus or a few smashed beans + pinch of garlic powder

1 tablespoon guacamole or a piece of smashed avocado + salt to taste

1 tablespoon plain 2 percent Greek yogurt + pinch of dried cilantro, basil, dill, or mint

1 tablespoon goat cheese + ½ teaspoon pesto (store-bought is fine)

1 teaspoon ricotta + ½ teaspoon spaghetti sauce

1½ teaspoons sour cream + 1½ teaspoons mayonnaise + a chopped black or green olive

1 tablespoon sour cream (or Greek yogurt) + pinch of taco seasoning

1 pint (285 g) cherry tomatoes, ideally in different colors, washed and with green leaves removed, if desired

Fill each section of a silicone or plastic ice cube tray with dip, mixing the dip recipes right in the tray. Place a whole tomato into the dip in each ice cube section (or quarter the tomatoes for kids under age three). Push fun toothpicks into each tomato, or let kids pierce them on their own!

All Kids Can . . .

- Wash and dry the tomatoes
- Remove the leaves from the tomatoes
- Fill the ice cube sections and mix the dips
- Push toothpicks into tomatoes and place a tomato in each section

Stuffed Cherry Tomatoes, Four Ways

TOTAL TIME: 20 to 30 minutes PREP: 20 to 30 minutes SERVES: 4

Kitchen tools such as colorful spatulas, light-up timers, whisks, and egg slicers are just toys for kids in the kitchen! For this recipe, they get to use melon ballers and piping bags (or a plastic bag with the corner cut off) to stuff roly-poly tomatoes four different ways. Be sure to use a melon baller with a smaller scoop (1 cm in diameter) for scooping out cherry tomatoes.

FILLING OPTION 1: HERBED CREAM CHEESE WITH CHIVES AND DILL

3 ounces (85 g) cream cheese, softened

2 tablespoons mayonnaise or plain 2 percent Greek yogurt

1 tablespoon minced fresh chives or finely chopped scallion, plus more for garnish (optional)

2 teaspoons minced fresh dill, plus more for garnish (optional)

FILLING OPTION 2: SWEET GOAT CHEESE

3 ounces (85 g) goat cheese, softened

2 tablespoons honey

Chopped walnuts for garnish (optional)

FILLING OPTION 3: SAVORY GOAT CHEESE

3 ounces (85 g) goat cheese, softened

2 teaspoons minced fresh basil

Dash of olive oil

Salt and black pepper to taste

Pine nuts, julienned fresh basil, or pinch of pink salt for garnish (optional)

FILLING OPTION 4: BRIE

3 ounces (85 g) Brie, softened

Pine nuts or julienned fresh basil for garnish (optional)

24 large cherry tomatoes (see Parenting in the Kitchen for serving toddlers)

① Mix the fillings in separate small bowls and allow them to rest to blend the flavors while you're scooping out the tomatoes.

② Carefully cut a thin slice off the bottom and top of each tomato (stem side). After slicing, place the tomatoes stem side down (upside down).

③ Using a small (1 cm) melon baller, scoop out the centers of each tomato, being careful not to cut into the bottom.

④ Simply using a small tasting spoon will get the job done, but kids love to pipe filling into the tomatoes. Use a pastry bag fitted with a small star tip, or fill a small plastic bag, snip off the corner, and squeeze.

⑤ Garnish, if desired, and serve.

All Kids Can . . .

- Wash and dry the tomatoes
- Remove the leaves from the tomatoes
- Scoop out the center of each tomato (with an adult's help)
- Chop the herbs with a kid-safe knife
- Mix the fillings
- Fill the piping bags and pipe filling into tomatoes
- Garnish the filled tomatoes

PARENTING IN THE KITCHEN

For kids under three, cut up a few hollowed-out tomatoes and let them dip those into the filling. Cherry tomatoes, even cut in half, can be a choking hazard until mouths are big enough to chomp down and control round foods for chewing and safe swallowing.

Mozzarella, Tomato, and Basil Stacks

TOTAL TIME: 20 minutes PREP: 15 minutes SERVES: 6

The traditional Italian combination of mozzarella, tomatoes, and basil is known as a caprese salad, but building towers of the creamy cheese and tart tomatoes is what makes it a "stack." You'll spark more interest in the construction process and handling large pieces of tomato by building them right at the dinner table.

4 large tomatoes, washed and sliced horizontally
9 ounces (250 g) buffalo mozzarella, sliced
16 fresh basil leaves
Olive oil for drizzling (optional)
Balsamic vinegar for drizzling (optional)
Pesto for drizzling (optional)
Sea salt

Everyone constructs their stacks at the table (see Parenting in the Kitchen to turn this into a contest). Drizzle with olive oil and balsamic vinegar, if using, or pesto, if preferred, and garnish with salt. (For an extra treat, try making the balsamic reduction described on page 197.)

All Kids Can . . .

- Wash and dry the tomatoes and basil
- Slice the mozzarella with a kid-safe knife
- Build stacks at the table
- Drizzle the oil, balsamic vinegar, and pesto
- Garnish with sea salt

Plus, Big Kids Can . . .

- Slice the tomatoes using a cat paw (see page 65)

PARENTING IN THE KITCHEN

Serving foods family style, where family members serve themselves from platters passed around the table, is a wonderful way to expose kids to new foods over time. But, if you'd like to encourage them to take food off the platter and put it on their plate, try this trick. Place the platters in easy reach of everyone on the table or place three smaller serving dishes of mozzarella, tomato, and basil in front of each person. Start a timer for 30 seconds as the youngest at the table says "Go!" Everyone at the table builds their stack using all three ingredients without letting them tumble. When the timer goes off, whoever has the tallest stack wins!

A Sweet Treat: Tomato Basil Sorbet

TOTAL TIME: 1 hour 15 minutes (includes 1 hour in the freezer)
PREP TIME: 15 minutes **MAKES:** 6 servings

Two or three whole tomatoes go into this sweet sorbet. The taste of basil is very subtle, so if you think you'd like a bit more oomph, add a pinch more.

1 cup (200 g) sugar
1 cup (240 ml) water
8 ounces (225 g) plum tomatoes (such as Roma)
1 cup (140 g) frozen red grapes
¼ teaspoon dried basil, crushed between your fingers to release oils
⅛ teaspoon salt

❶ To make a simple syrup, combine the sugar and water in a medium saucepan. Stir over medium heat until the sugar dissolves. Raise the heat to high and bring to a boil, then reduce the heat to medium and simmer for 3 minutes. Pour ¾ cup (180 ml) of the syrup into a blender and allow it to cool to room temperature. Reserve the remainder should you need to thin down the sorbet while blending.

❷ While the simple syrup is cooling, seed the tomatoes and chop them into small chunks. Discard the seeds. Add the tomatoes, grapes, basil, and salt to the syrup and blend until only small flecks of tomato and grape skins remain.

❸ Pour the mixture into six 6-ounce (30 ml) ramekins and freeze for 1 hour before serving.

- Wash and dry the tomatoes
- Seed and chop the tomatoes using a kid-safe knife
- Crush the dried basil
- Add the ingredients to the blender
- Turn the blender on and off
  (with adult supervision)

Plus, Big Kids Can . . .

- Make the simple syrup
  (with adult supervision)

Part Four

AUTUMN VEGETABLES

The fall is my favorite time of year for exploring new vegetables. Crops include hearty veggies like brussels sprouts, cabbage, and kale. It's as if nature is preparing us for winter, providing us with vegetables that have a bit more substance to them and are foods we can really sink our teeth into! Many of the fall crops can be found in stores year-round, providing lots of opportunities to use them in a variety of dishes and learn to love them over time. Start with the ideas in this book, but then branch out and try other recipes. Keep cooking with your kids and continue to expose, explore, expand. Do you have other family recipes to share with your kids? If not, you're creating them now, and they'll be passed down from generation to generation. It takes time, but the memories you'll create in the kitchen will be worth it.

BRUSSELS SPROUTS

Along with the antioxidant vitamin K, brussels sprouts have glucosinolates, which keep our heart healthy. Brussels sprouts look like cute mini cabbages that grow on a stalk, one upon another hiding beneath large, edible leaves. Depending on the variety, a mature stalk has twenty to forty sprouts. If you're growing your own, try sautéing the large leaves just like the beet greens on page 20. Fresh from the garden, unwashed sprouts can be stored for a few days in plastic bags in the refrigerator. If stored longer, they gradually become bitter. That's why I always buy just enough fresh B-sprouts for one recipe at a time. Look for ones that have tightly packed leaves for optimum freshness. My favorites are the tiniest ones, which are sweeter and, well, even cuter!

EXPOSE

Race to the Finish

No matter what the age, I've never met a kid who didn't relish beating me in this race. For kids under the age of three who are still practicing their fine motor skills, buy a few older sprouts that have looser leaves, just to give them a head start. (Toss those sprouts afterward. They just aren't fresh enough to be tasty.)

What you'll need:

- Small bowl of different-sized brussels sprouts, washed and patted dry
- Digital timer (or a visual timer for younger kids, like an hourglass sand timer)

What to do:

1 PARENTS: Set the timer for 1, 2, or 3 minutes. (Don't tell the other players what you set.) When you start the timer and shout "Go!" every player grabs a brussels sprout from the bowl. Players peel one leaf at time until the timer rings. Options for winning: 1) The person with the most leaves peeled off the sprout wins; 2) the first person to peel all his leaves wins; 3) the person with the tiniest whole leaf wins. (Use a timer even if it's not needed, just to encourage kids to work quickly. Otherwise, they may take their time slowly peeling off one outer leaf and may not get much exposure to the rest of the sprout.)

2 PARENTS AND KIDS: When the game is over, rinse the leaves, pat them dry, and save them for upcoming recipes such as Brussels Sprout Salad (page 198) and Sprinkles and Sprouts (page 200), unless you're using older sprouts for the younger kids, as mentioned above.

How your child benefits

Fine motor skills are key for this game, as kids quickly yet carefully peel each leaf. Kids will also be problem solving, since they must plan ahead and develop a strategy before they hear "Go!" Should they grab a big sprout or a smaller sprout? It will depend on the goal: For instance, are they trying to finish peeling first or to finish with the most whole leaves?

Penne with Brussels Sprouts

TOTAL TIME: 45 to 50 minutes PREP: 20 minutes COOK: 25 to 30 minutes
SERVES: 6 as an entrée

Three tricks are useful for introducing the flavor of brussels sprouts to kids: 1) Roast them, 2) shave them, or 3) combine them with pasta. This recipe does all three!

1 pound (455 g) penne pasta (gluten-free if needed)
25 small to medium brussels sprouts, washed and trimmed
1 medium red onion, chopped
4 tablespoons extra virgin olive oil, plus more if needed
Salt and black pepper to taste
2 tablespoons chopped fresh sage
1 teaspoon minced garlic
2 ounces (55 g) Parmesan, shaved, plus more for garnish
3 tablespoons pesto (optional; store-bought is fine)

1 Boil water in a large pot for the pasta and cook per the package directions.

2 Preheat the oven to 400°F (200°C).

3 In a food processor, shave the brussels sprouts using the slicing disk.

4 In a medium bowl, toss the shaved brussels sprouts with the onion and 2 tablespoons of the oil, until the veggies are lightly coated. Add a bit more oil if needed.

5 Spread the veggie mix evenly on a baking sheet and roast for 20 minutes, or until the edges of the sprouts begin to brown.

6 Drain the cooked pasta and return it to the warm pasta pot. Add the remaining 2 tablespoons oil, toss to lightly coat the pasta, and season lightly with salt and pepper.

7 Remove the baking sheet from the oven momentarily to add the sage, garlic, and salt and pepper to the mix. Stir the sprouts and seasonings together, then spread across the baking sheet once more. Put the baking sheet back in the oven for 5 to 10 more minutes, until the sprouts are lightly crisped and browned a bit more.

8 Stir the brussels sprouts mixture into the pasta. Add the Parmesan and stir to melt. Stir in the pesto, if desired. Serve warm with a few more Parmesan shavings on top.

All Kids Can . . .

- Wash and dry the brussels sprouts
- Cut off the ends of the brussels sprouts with a kid-safe knife
- Drop the brussels sprouts into the chute of the food processor (with an adult's help)
- Turn the food processor on and off (with adult supervision)
- Add salt and pepper to taste
- Add Parmesan shavings to the top of the pasta before serving

Plus, Big Kids Can . . .

- Chop the onion with a sharp knife (with adult supervision)
- Boil water and cook the pasta (with adult supervision)
- Stir in new ingredients at each stage of the recipe

KITCHEN SCIENCE

Why does roasting make bitter vegetables taste nutty and sweet? As vegetables roast in the oven, they release water (as steam) and their complex starches are broken down into simple sugars, which re-form into other sugars and turn progressively browner. That process, called caramelization, results in a sweet, caramel-like flavor.

Brussels Sprout and Grape Kebabs

TOTAL TIME: 40 minutes **PREP:** 20 minutes **COOK:** 20 minutes **MAKES:** 8 kebabs

Cooking with skewers is always fun! You'll need eight short skewers for spearing the brussels sprouts and grapes that are roasted together in this kebab recipe. If you're using wooden skewers, soak them in water for 15 minutes before using them.

12 small brussels sprouts, washed and trimmed
12 large, firm seedless red grapes
Olive oil for drizzling
1 tablespoon chopped fresh thyme
¼ cup (60 ml) balsamic vinegar
1 tablespoon honey
Sea salt to taste

1. Preheat the oven to 400°F (200°C).

2. Cut the brussels sprouts in half, lengthwise, saving any loose leaves for Brussels Sprout Salad (page 198) or Sprinkles and Sprouts (page 200). Put all the brussels sprouts flat-side down on a cutting board.

3. Cut the grapes in half lengthwise.

4. Spear a brussels sprout half on a skewer and then spear a grape half, arranging them so the flat side of the grape is against the flat side of the brussels sprout.

5. Repeat this pattern, sliding sprouts and grapes into place until each skewer has three pieces of grape and three pieces of brussels sprout. Place each kebab on a baking sheet as it's assembled.

6. Drizzle olive oil lightly over the skewers and sprinkle the thyme on top.

⑦ Roast the kebabs for 20 minutes, or until the brussels sprouts are softened and browned slightly.

⑧ While the kebabs are in the oven, stir the balsamic vinegar and honey together in a small saucepan over high heat. Bring the mixture to a boil and reduce the heat to low. Simmer until the mixture is reduced and thickened slightly, 3 to 5 minutes. Remove the pan from the heat and allow the reduction to cool until the kebabs are ready.

⑨ Remove the cooked kebabs from the oven, allow them to cool slightly, then place them on a plate and drizzle the balsamic reduction on top. Season with salt and serve.

All Kids Can . . .

- Soak the skewers
- Wash and dry the brussels sprouts
- Cut the ends off the brussels sprouts with a kid-safe knife
- Cut the grapes in half with a kid-safe knife
- Chop the thyme (or use kid-safe scissors)
- Spear the grapes and brussels sprouts
- Drizzle the olive oil
- Sprinkle the thyme
- Arrange the skewers on a baking sheet

PARENTING IN THE KITCHEN

Toddlers will definitely need a parent's help and attention in handling these skewers and the round pieces. Halved, roasted grapes are not a choking concern (unlike fresh grapes), but the brussels sprouts may need to be cut or pulled apart for kids younger than three, unless they're cooked until very, very tender.

Brussels Sprout Salad

TOTAL TIME: **40 minutes** (including time to let the salad sit and soften) SERVES: **8**

The best thing about this salad—besides its amazing flavor—is that leftovers keep in the refrigerator for up to two days and the extra dressing for even longer. I can make the salad the day before, which really lets the flavors blend, or serve it right away and snack on the leftovers the next day. My daughters are all grown up now, but when they come to visit and I see them snacking on the leftover salad, I still get a swelling of pride. It feels good to raise healthy eaters.

DIJON MUSTARD DRESSING

¾ cup (180 ml) vegetable oil

3 tablespoons extra virgin olive oil

2 to 3 tablespoons champagne vinegar

1 to 2 teaspoons fresh lemon juice

1 teaspoon Dijon or whole grain mustard

⅛ teaspoon minced garlic

Salt and black pepper to taste

SALAD

8 ounces (225 g) brussels sprouts, washed, dried, and trimmed

3 tablespoons dried cherries, cranberries, or golden raisins (or 1 tablespoon of each)

2 tablespoons sliced smoked almonds

Parmesan shavings for garnish

❶ To make the Dijon Mustard Dressing, whisk the oils together in a glass measuring cup. In a bowl, whisk the remaining dressing ingredients together. Drizzle the oil mixture into the bowl, whisking until all the dressing ingredients are combined.

❷ To make the Salad, pull off as many leaves of the brussels sprouts as you can and put them in a salad bowl. Chop off any remaining stems and discard. Chop the interior and remaining leaves of the brussels sprouts into pea-sized pieces and add those to the salad bowl.

3 Add the dried cherries, almonds, and about a third of the dressing (be careful not to overdo it—you don't want a soggy salad) to the salad bowl and toss with the pieces and leaves of the brussels sprouts until everything is coated. Let the salad sit for 10 minutes to soften. Add more dressing if desired, and serve on individual plates with Parmesan shavings on top.

4 Store the remaining dressing in an airtight container in the refrigerator for up to five days to add to any leftover salad. The leaves tend to soak up the last drops of the dressing, which makes for an extra yummy salad the next day!

All Kids Can . . .

- Wash and dry the brussels sprouts
- Cut off the ends of the brussels sprouts with a kid-safe knife
- Squeeze the lemon juice
- Whisk the dressing
- Pull the leaves off the brussels sprouts
- Toss the salad
- Garnish with Parmesan shavings

A Sweet Treat: Sprinkles and Sprouts

TOTAL TIME: **25 minutes** PREP: **10 minutes** COOK: **10 to 15 minutes** SERVES: **4 as a dessert**

A dash of rainbow sprinkles makes these tempting to taste and adds an extra crunch, too! Roasting the leaves of the brussels sprouts brings out the natural sweetness of the veggie, and the unexpected sprinkles add a touch of whimsy. I once served these to a group of adults, and they were giggling as they ate them. This recipe brings out the kid in all of us!

Outermost leaves from 2 pounds (905 g) brussels sprouts
Olive oil for drizzling
Salt and black pepper to taste
Rainbow sprinkles

1 Preheat the oven to 400°F (200°C).

2 Toss the brussels sprout leaves on a baking sheet with just a drizzle of olive oil and some salt and pepper. Gently massage the oil into the leaves with your clean fingers.

3 Scatter the leaves on the sheet in a single layer and roast for 10 to 15 minutes, until each leaf is slightly brown on the edges. You may need to remove smaller leaves (which will brown more quickly) from the pan before the larger leaves have become crispy.

4 Sprinkle with the rainbow sprinkles and enjoy!

All Kids Can . . .

- Wash and dry the brussels sprouts
- Pull the outermost leaves off the brussels sprouts
- Spread the brussels sprouts on a baking sheet
- Drizzle the brussels sprouts with oil
- Sprinkle the rainbow sprinkles

PARENTING IN THE KITCHEN

You'll find that most of the sweet treats in this book are lower in sugar than many dessert recipes. Teach kids how to enjoy sugar in moderation: Keep portions small and don't offer dessert every night. Consider serving a tiny piece of dessert *with* dinner. When a small piece of a sweet treat is included on the dinner plate (rather than afterward), it's yet *another* special food on the plate—along with, for instance, the delicious brussels sprouts. (Brussels sprouts are always special in my mind, just like sprinkles!)

Oops! Sprinkles go on *after* roasting! This cutie-patootie just could not wait!

CABBAGE

"The time has come," the Walrus said,
"To talk of many things:
Of shoes—and ships—and sealing-wax—
Of cabbages—and kings..."

"The Walrus and the Carpenter," the beloved poem by
Lewis Carroll, is actually a story about the main characters
preparing to have a feast of raw oysters! We won't be quite that adventurous
in these recipes, but we will be eating brains.... You'll see what I mean in the
upcoming Explore section. Here's a brain-smart fact about cabbage: It has
vitamin K and sulforaphane, which give us first-class blood that pumps through
our whole body to keep our brain sharp so we can pay thinking games—like
Cabbage Bingo!

EXPOSE

Cabbage Bingo

Kids will get a kick out of making a bingo board from cabbage leaves! One head of cabbage
should provide enough leaves for up to four players.

What you'll need:

- 1 head fresh green or red cabbage
- Clean hole puncher
- One sheet of poster board or white paper
  for each player, at least 8½ × 11 inches
  (21.5 × 28 cm)

- One die for rolling numbers
- 15 raspberries, blackberries, or other
  small soft fruit for each player
- Scissors
- Colored marker

What to do:

1 **PARENTS:** Peel apart the cabbage leaves, being careful not to tear them. Wash and pat them dry. Cut the leaves into halves or quarters, depending on the size of the cabbage.

2 **PARENTS AND KIDS:** Using the hole puncher, randomly punch one to six holes as close to the center of each leaf as possible, to represent the numbers 1 through 6 Sometimes the leaves can be folded gently to make two holes with each punch. (This is a terrific time to give cabbage a taste test—just pop one of the tiny circles just punched out of the cabbage right into your mouth!)

3 **PARENTS:** On each sheet of paper, write the letters B, I, N, G, O spread evenly across the top of the long side. Draw lines down the short side of the board, creating columns for a BINGO board. Each player gets fifteen leaves of cabbage, with three leaves under each letter. (You can use five leaves of cabbage under each letter for older kids. Three is plenty for the younger ages.)

4 **PARENTS AND KIDS:** Randomly place cabbage leaves under each letter on each playing board. Take turns calling out B, I, N, G, or O and roll the die to add on the number 1, 2, 3, 4, 5, or 6. Each player places a piece of fruit in the leaf when it matches the letter and number of holes called out. The first person who gets their fruit in a straight horizontal line wins! (Children playing on a 5 × 5 board can win with straight vertical or diagonal lines, too.)

How your child benefits

Kids learn to recognize holes in the leaf as a number while paying attention to verbal directions and visual input at the same time. For the youngest players, limiting the winning combination to a horizontal line (rather than down the page or at a diagonal) encourages visual tracking from left to right for early reading skills. By giving each child a turn at calling out the letters and rolling the die, they practice letter recall and memory for letters and numbers—skills that are the foundation for reading and math. And it's no small thing that they are also having fun with cabbage—which can be a foundation for wanting to eat it!

Grilled Cabbage Brains

TOTAL TIME: 40 minutes PREP: 10 minutes COOK: 10 minutes per batch on the grill SERVES: 6

Calling a food a really disgusting name like "brains" is almost always a hit with preschoolers. They giggle and laugh, yelling out "I'm eating brains!" These slices of cabbage resemble the swirls and crevices found in the human brain and are loaded with brain food like vitamin K and flavonoids, which help with concentration. So eat your brains—it will make you smarter.

¼ cup (60 ml) plus 1 tablespoon avocado oil
½ small shallot, chopped
1 tablespoon white balsamic vinegar
2 teaspoons Dijon mustard
1 teaspoon honey
Salt and black pepper to taste
1 medium green cabbage

1 Whisk ¼ cup (60 ml) of the oil, the shallot, vinegar, mustard, honey, salt, and pepper together to make a dressing.

2 Heat a grill pan on medium heat. Add the remaining 1 tablespoon oil and spread it evenly across the surface of the hot pan.

3 Remove the outermost leaves of the cabbage and discard them. Slice the head of cabbage into ¾-inch (2 cm) rounds or half rounds and carefully place on the grill pan.

4 Grill the cabbage for 3 minutes, then lightly drizzle with some of the dressing. The dressing will seep through the cabbage and help with caramelization on the other side. (For more about caramelization, see page 195.) Grill until the cabbage is slightly browned and lightly softened, about 2 more minutes. Don't overcook it, or the "brains" will fall apart. Carefully flip with a spatula. If they separate a bit when flipping, simply use the spatula to push them back into the intended shape.

⑤ Grill the cabbage on the second side for 3 minutes, then lightly drizzle with more dressing. Grill for 2 more minutes to brown that side.

⑥ Transfer the brains carefully to a serving platter and drizzle them with the remaining dressing just before serving.

All Kids Can . . .

- Wash and dry the cabbage

- Slice the cabbage into "brains" with a kid-safe knife (with an adult's help)
- Whisk the dressing
- Drizzle the remaining dressing just before serving

Plus, Big Kids Can . . .

- Help at the grill, flipping the cabbage with adult supervision

Cabbage, Carrot, and Jicama Wraps

TOTAL TIME: 45 minutes PREP: 25 minutes MAKES: 10 spring rolls

Kids adore making these summer rolls, filled with their favorite julienned veggies! Dip them in peanut sauce (or a nut-free variation) for a bit of protein, or add shredded chicken to the wrap. How about setting out all the ingredients and just watching to see what your kids create? Half the joy is the creation; the other half is the crunch!

PEANUT (OR NUT-FREE) SAUCE

2 tablespoons extra virgin olive oil

2 tablespoons honey

1 tablespoon lemon or lime juice, plus more to taste

1 tablespoon rice vinegar

1 teaspoon coconut aminos, soy sauce, or tamari (gluten-free if needed), plus more if desired

⅛ teaspoon garlic powder

¼ cup (65 g) creamy peanut butter (use sunflower seed butter for nut-free sauce)

WRAPS

1 large carrot, peeled and julienned

1 medium jicama, peeled and julienned

⅓ cup (35 g) chopped red cabbage (pieces should be the size of confetti)

2 tablespoons chopped fresh cilantro, mint, or basil

5 butter lettuce leaves, torn in half

10 summer roll rice paper wrappers (found in the international section of grocery stores)

OPTIONAL ADDITIONS

1 avocado, halved, pitted, and sliced

1 cup (100 g) bean sprouts

½ English cucumber, julienned

½ red or yellow bell pepper, julienned

5 scallions, julienned

Shredded chicken (see Tip on page 92)

① To make the Peanut Sauce, whisk together the oil, honey, lemon juice, vinegar, coconut aminos, and garlic

powder in a microwave-safe bowl. Stir in the peanut butter and microwave on high for 10 to 20 seconds to warm the mixture. (This step is essential for blending in the peanut butter.) Whisk again, blending all the ingredients. Taste and add additional lemon juice or coconut aminos, if desired.

② Display all the wrap ingredients within easy reach on the counter to begin assembly.

③ Pour some warm water into a large shallow bowl or a round cake pan large enough to fit a wrapper. Moisten a wrapper, following the package directions—typically they need to be dipped in water for 15 to 20 seconds—and being careful that it doesn't become so soft that it won't hold the fillings.

④ Place the wrapper on a cutting board and pat it dry. Lay a few julienned carrots and jicama on the bottom third of the wrapper. Add small amounts of the optional additions if desired. Sprinkle with some cabbage confetti and cilantro. Cover the filling with a lettuce leaf half. (The leaf helps keep the wrapper from tearing as you roll it up, but it is not a must if kids balk at lettuce.)

⑤ To roll, fold the bottom edge of the wrapper up and over the filling, then continue rolling, carefully but tightly, folding in the sides of the wrapper as you go.

⑥ Cut the wrapper in half and at an angle. Serve with a small dish of the Peanut Sauce for dipping.

All Kids Can . . .

- Wash and dry all the veggies
- Whisk the ingredients for the sauce
- Microwave the peanut butter (with an adult's help)
- Tear the lettuce leaves in half
- Cut the avocado with a kid-safe knife
- Set up a display of all the ingredients, ready for assembly
- Dip the wrapping papers into the water
- Wrap the veggies into a roll (with an adult's help)

Plus, Big Kids Can . . .

- Peel the carrots and jicama (with adult supervision)
- Julienne the carrots and jicama and optional veggies (with adult supervision)
- Use a food processor to make cabbage confetti (with adult supervision)

Polish Cabbage Rolls (Pigs in a Blanket)

TOTAL TIME: **1½ hours** PREP: **20 minutes** SERVES: **8**

This recipe is from occupational therapist Judy Delaware. I depend on OTs when I need to understand the finer points of each child's unique sensory system, which is their specialty. Judy is of Polish descent, and she couldn't pass up the opportunity to share her family's recipe for Polish stuffed cabbage, a dish filled with lovely aromas and offering various flavors and textures—all sensory aspects of food that make this meal delectable in every way. This dish is even better the next day. The entire pot can be reheated, or a few cabbage rolls can be warmed in the microwave.

2 cups (385 g) medium-grain white rice

4 cups (960 ml) water

3 teaspoons salt

1 pound (455 g) lean ground beef or pork (or low-fat turkey sausage or Polish sausage that has been ground to the consistency of coarse taco meat)

1 small onion, chopped

1 teaspoon black pepper

1 medium to large frozen cabbage (see Tip), thawed on the kitchen counter overnight

Two 8-ounce (227 g) cans tomato sauce

2 tablespoons light brown sugar

1 Cook the rice in the water with 1 teaspoon of the salt, according to the package directions or in a rice cooker. Keep warm.

2 Meanwhile, brown the beef in a medium skillet over medium heat until it's cooked thoroughly. Remove the meat from the pan, leaving some of the fat.

3 Cook the chopped onion in the fat from the meat until golden brown. Transfer the onion and fat to the rice. Add the beef and pepper and the remaining 2 teaspoons salt. Mix everything together well.

4 Separate the leaves and remove the tough leaf stems from the head of cabbage. Some of the inner leaves may be too small for using as wrappers. Lay these in the

bottom of a heavy-bottomed pot that is also oven-safe (a Dutch oven is perfect).

5 Take a cabbage leaf and place 2 or 3 tablespoons of the rice and meat mixture on the leaf near the stem end in a mound. (This amount is an estimate, since the size of the leaves can vary. If you're making these cabbage rolls for smaller hands, make the mounds smaller.)

6 Roll the stem end over to cover the mixture. Then fold both sides of the cabbage leaf, one at a time, over to the center as if making an envelope. Roll the entire mound tightly toward the end. Use toothpicks to pin the cabbage roll together for cooking. Place the cabbage roll the pot so that the seam side is facing down.

7 Repeat this process until all the filling is used up, making sure to fit the stuffed rolls tightly up against each other in the pot to prevent them from floating while cooking.

8 Add water to the pot until the cabbage rolls are 1 inch (2.5 cm) below the surface of the liquid. Put the pot on the stove, bring to a boil, then lower the heat and simmer gently for 30 minutes with the lid of the pot half on and half off. There should still be some water at the bottom of the pot after 30 minutes of cooking.

9 Preheat the oven to 350°F (180°C).

10 Mix the tomato sauce and brown sugar. Pour over the cabbage rolls. Cover and place the pot in the oven and bake for 1 hour. The rolls are done when they feel soft to the touch of a wooden spoon and the sauce is bubbling.

All Kids Can . . .

- Wash, dry, and freeze the cabbage
- Pull the leaves off the cabbage to use for the rolls
- Make the rice (with an adult's help)
- Fill and fold the cabbage rolls (with an adult's help)
- Mix the sauce and pour it over the cabbage rolls

Plus, Big Kids Can . . .

- Cook the beef (with adult supervision)
- Place the cabbage rolls in the pot with water and bring to a boil (with adult supervision)

TIP

Freezing a head of cabbage will make the leaves peel away more easily. Remove any dirty or blackened outer leaves. Place the cabbage on a cutting board. Trim off any bit of stem to reveal the core. Stick a fork in the core to stabilize the cabbage as you cut In a circle around the core and then pull out the core. Wrap the head in heavy-duty plastic and freeze for 24 hours.

A Sweet Treat: Cabbage Cupcakes

TOTAL TIME: 45 minutes PREP: 25 minutes MAKES: 18 to 24 cupcakes

These pretty little cakes are reminiscent of traditional carrot cake, but they have red cabbage to make them ultramoist. Add a candle to each one before serving, and let everyone make a wish before blowing out their candles. After all, it's somebody's birthday, somewhere! Why not celebrate?

2¼ cups (280 g) all-purpose flour (gluten-free if needed)
1½ cups (300 g) granulated sugar
2 teaspoons baking soda
2 teaspoons ground cinnamon
¼ teaspoon ground nutmeg
¼ teaspoon salt
1 cup (240 ml) canola oil
¾ cup (180 ml) buttermilk
3 large eggs
3 teaspoons pure vanilla extract
1 cup (280 g) plain 2 percent Greek yogurt
¾ cup plus 3 tablespoons (95 g) finely chopped red cabbage (a food processor works well)
¾ cup (95 g) chopped pecans
½ cup (55g) shredded carrot
¼ cup (25 g) unsweetened coconut flakes
¼ cup (40 g) raisins

CREAM CHEESE FROSTING

8 ounces (225 g) cream cheese, at room temperature
5½ tablespoons (80 g) unsalted butter, at room temperature
4 cups (480 g) confectioner's sugar
2 teaspoons pure vanilla extract

1 Preheat the oven to 350°F (180°C). Spray two muffin pans with nonstick cooking spray or line with baking cups.

2 In a medium bowl, sift together the flour, granulated sugar, baking soda, cinnamon, nutmeg, and salt.

3 Using a stand or handheld mixer, blend the oil, buttermilk, eggs, and vanilla extract.

4 Add the dry mixture to the wet and mix on low speed, scraping the side of the bowl with a rubber spatula to make sure everything is well incorporated. Increase the mixer speed to medium for 20 seconds, while adding the yogurt and blending until creamy.

5 Fold in the cabbage, pecans, carrots, coconut flakes, and raisins and distribute evenly. Do not overmix.

6 Fill the muffin cups halfway and bake for 15 to 18 minutes, until a toothpick inserted in the middle of a cupcake comes out clean. Remove the pans from the oven and transfer the cupcakes to a wire rack to cool.

7 To make the Cream Cheese Frosting, beat the cream cheese and butter until well blended. Add the confectioners' sugar and vanilla. Beat until creamy.

8 Top each cupcake with a dollop of Cream Cheese Frosting (see Tip).

All Kids Can . . .

- Wash and dry all the veggies
- Spray the muffin pans or line them with baking cups
- Chop the cabbage and carrots in a food processor (with an adult's help)
- Sift the dry ingredients
- Blend the wet ingredients (with an adult's help)
- Add the dry mixture to the wet one
- Fold in the other ingredients
- Fill the muffin pans with batter (with an adult's help)
- Mix the frosting (with an adult's help)
- Frost the cupcakes (always lick the spoon!)

TIP

What's up with this new trend of cupcakes that have a mountain of frosting on top? For this treat, just put a small swirl or a dollop (add some sprinkles, too, if you'd like to make it fancy) and make the cupcake the star of the show. Less sugar, more cabbage!

CAULIFLOWER

White, green, purple, and orange: Create a bouquet of this sweet, crunchy, cruciferous vegetable! (Other well-known cruciferous vegetables include cabbage, broccoli, kale, brussels sprouts, and collard greens.) All four colors taste similar, but the purple and orange "cauli" have more antioxidants, so I try to buy those whenever I can. Cauliflower is superb for heart health, detoxification, and digestion. It packs a 1-2-3 punch!

EXPOSE

Cauliflower Sheep

Try orange, green, purple, and white cauliflower to make sheep that come in every color, or mix them up to create a new breed of rainbow sheep. The wonderful thing about vegetable crafts is there really are no rules. It's all about creativity!

What you'll need:

- Fresh cauliflower (at least one head per person if everyone shares pieces of various colors)
- Wooden skewers cut to desired lengths
- Thick toothpicks

- Raisins
- Pitted black or green olives
- Small scissors or child-safe knives for trimming olives and skewers

What to do:

1 KIDS: Wash any dirt off the cauliflower. With a cutting board on a sturdy surface, hold the head of the cauliflower up high and smash the stem or core of the cauliflower *hard* on the cutting board. Wiggle the core and it will pop right out! Break off florets in a variety of sizes and shapes. Use larger pieces for the sheep's body and cut pieces of the stem for legs. Connect everything with skewers and toothpicks. Raisins can be threaded onto toothpicks for hooves or olives can be trimmed to make ears. Or craft a fancy bow tie or top hat: For a top hat, just slice the olive in half and cut another thin slice for the hat's brim. Put the brim on the head first, then stack the half olive on top of that and fasten both with one toothpick through the top. Bow ties are easy too—just slice the olive from end to end and cut two triangles off of each side to form a bow shape. Fasten with a toothpick to the sheep, anywhere you think it needs a bow.

2 PARENTS: For the younger set, blanch and cool the cauliflower florets to make it easy for little hands to insert the skewers (see blanching instructions on page 81). Be sure to monitor small children while helping them construct the animal and hand them one raisin or olive at a time so that they don't pop a bunch in their mouths. Round foods and clumped raisins can be a choking hazard, but that doesn't mean we should avoid them altogether, especially in food play. Older kids may get quite creative making all sorts of animals; you'll be astonished at what they craft with just a few raisins, olives, and cauliflower. Be sure to join in—that's half the fun of kitchen projects with kids.

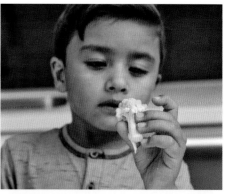

How your child benefits

As kids interact with the cauliflower, they are also practicing fine motor skills that are often missed in today's world of technology and excessive digital media use by children. In the process of making adorable herds of sheep, your child is practicing different types of grasps, depending on the size of the food they are holding. Learning to manipulate the hand, turn the wrist, and press skewers into various textures of food requires eye-hand coordination and a specific grading of movement that's delicate yet strong! Visual skills like visual scanning (searching for a certain sized piece), visual discrimination (How does this size fit with the image in my brain?), and visual memory (What do I need to do next?) all come into play. Cognitive skills include problem solving (What do I do when a piece accidently breaks?) and math skills (How many of these do I need to make ears, legs, or a tail?). Combine all of this with a dash of imagination and it's a recipe for raising one smart and resourceful child.

Striped Cauliflower Gratin

TOTAL TIME: 45 to 50 minutes PREP: 25 minutes COOK: 20 to 25 minutes
MAKES: 8 large portions

Use orange and white cauliflower chopped into pieces about the size of macaroni elbows to resemble fancy striped mac 'n' cheese! It's just as tasty, but much healthier and boosted with fiber, protein, and vitamin C. Surprisingly, this recipe contains more calcium than the pasta version, thanks to . . . can you guess? Cauliflower.

Butter for greasing the baking dish
2 cups (480 ml) vegetable or chicken broth
1 small head orange cauliflower, chopped into macaroni-elbow-sized pieces
1 small head white cauliflower, chopped into macaroni-elbow-sized pieces
1½ cups (340 g) plain 2 percent Greek yogurt
2 teaspoons Dijon mustard
2 teaspoons salt
1 teaspoon black pepper
⅔ cup (75 g) shredded mozzarella
⅓ cup (37 g) shredded medium-sharp cheddar
½ cup (55 g) shredded Parmesan
¼ cup (25 g) dried bread crumbs (optional; gluten-free if needed)

1 Preheat the oven to 375°F (190°C). Butter a 12 × 8-inch (30 × 20 cm) baking dish.

2 In two medium saucepans, divide the broth and bring to a boil. Add orange cauliflower to one pan and white to the other. Turn the heat down to a simmer, stirring occasionally until the cauliflower is tender, about 10 minutes. Drain each color separately.

3 While the cauliflower is cooking, mix the yogurt, mustard, salt, and pepper in a large bowl, then pour half of the mixture into another large bowl.

④ Stir the orange cauliflower into one bowl of the yogurt mixture and the white cauliflower into the other.

⑤ Loosely combine the mozzarella and cheddar, then fold half of the cheese mixture into each bowl of cauliflower.

⑥ Spoon one third of the white cauliflower mixture into the baking dish, lining the mixture against one short side. Spoon a third of the orange cauliflower mixture into the baking dish, lining that mixture up against the white strip of cauliflower. Continue this pattern until the dish is filled.

⑦ Sprinkle the Parmesan and bread crumbs (if using) on top of the cauliflower. Bake for 20 to 25 minutes, until the top is golden brown. Serve warm.

All Kids Can . . .

- Butter the baking dish
- Wash and dry the cauliflower
- Chop the cauliflower with a kid-safe knife

- Combine the yogurt and seasonings
- Stir the cauliflower into the yogurt mixture
- Spoon the mixture into the baking dish, creating stripes
- Sprinkle Parmesan (and bread crumbs, if using)

Plus, Big Kids Can . . .

- Cook the cauliflower (with adult supervision)

PARENTING IN THE KITCHEN

Kids find comfort in "sameness." How often do you hear "But I just want mac 'n' cheese!"? For hesitant eaters, change a favorite dish just slightly over time. You might mix in some of the pasta they love in mac 'n' cheese with the white cauliflower in this dish, encouraging them to alternate the stripes of orange cauliflower with the white pasta-cauliflower mix. By getting them involved in the process of creating the dish, they will adjust to the change over time.

Cinnamon Cream of Cauliflower Soup with Sweet Homemade Croutons

TOTAL TIME: **1 hour** PREP: **20 minutes** COOK: **40 minutes** MAKES: **6 cups (1.4 L)**

This soup is slightly sweet, with spices reminiscent of the holidays . . . oh, so comforting on a snowy winter day! And whether the sweet maple croutons are eaten alongside the soup or sprinkled on top, they add just a bit of crunch to complement the warm creaminess of the soup.

CINNAMON CREAM OF CAULIFLOWER SOUP

2 tablespoons coconut oil

1 medium head white cauliflower, cored and coarsely chopped

1 small yellow or red onion, chopped

4 cups (960 ml) chicken or vegetable broth

2 large apples, peeled, cored, and diced (Braeburn, Fuji, or Gala are the ideal sweetness)

2 teaspoons salt

1 teaspoon ground cinnamon

½ teaspoon ground cloves

½ teaspoon ground ginger

2 tablespoons coconut cream

2 teaspoons honey

SWEET HOMEMADE CROUTONS

1 tablespoon melted coconut oil

1 teaspoon pure maple syrup

1 teaspoon ground cinnamon

3 slices of your preferred sandwich bread (stale bread is ideal), cut into 1-inch (2.5 cm) cubes

To make the Cinnamon Cream of Cauliflower Soup, melt the oil in a large, heavy soup pot over medium heat. Add the cauliflower and onion and cook until softened slightly. Add the broth, apples, salt, cinnamon, cloves,

and ginger and simmer for about 20 minutes, until the vegetables and apples are tender.

② To make the Sweet Homemade Croutons, preheat the oven to 350°F (180°C). Mix the oil, maple syrup, and cinnamon together in a large bowl. Toss the bread cubes in the oil mixture, coating evenly.

③ Spread the cubes on a baking sheet, leaving space between the cubes for even browning. Bake for 10 to 15 minutes, until the cubes are browned on one side. Turn the cubes over for final browning on the other side for 2 to 3 minutes. Remove them from the oven and allow to cool.

④ Remove the soup from the heat. Stir in the coconut cream and honey until dissolved. Use an immersion blender (or allow to cool and use a regular blender) to puree.

⑤ Return the soup to the pot, gradually bring it back to temperature, then serve in small bowls or teacups with croutons on top.

All Kids Can . . .

- Wash and dry the cauliflower and apples
- Chop the cauliflower with a kid-safe knife
- Mix and toss the flavored oil with the bread cubes
- Spread the cubes on a baking sheet
- Add the soup ingredients to the pot (with an adult's help)

Plus, Big Kids Can . . .

- Bake the croutons (with adult supervision)
- Chop the onion (with adult supervision)
- Cook the ingredients in the soup pot (with adult supervision)
- Use the immersion blender (with adult supervision)

PARENTING IN THE KITCHEN

One trick to helping kids learn to love all kinds of soups is to offer tiny portions with a very short straw. My favorite miniature soup bowl is an espresso cup or teacup. The smaller size keeps the soup at a "just right" temperature for young kids, and the short straw allows a "just right" amount to land on their tongue with each sip. On top of that, this serving method means less mess when kids are still not adept at using a spoon.

Cauliflower Fried Rice

TOTAL TIME: 20 to 25 minutes PREP: 15 minutes COOK: 5 to 10 minutes
SERVES: 4 to 6 as a side dish

Kids get plenty of carbs, so finding a substitute that's healthier and more nutritious is essential for growing bodies. Learning to rice cauliflower is an exciting activity for kids and gets them involved right from the start. White cauliflower is ideal for this recipe, especially if you decide to use half traditional rice and half riced cauliflower. That combination is a great place to start with the more hesitant eater. For a subtle change in color, try brown rice. For the more adventurous eater, try ricing several of the colored varieties of cauliflower together for a vibrant twist! This dish gets a strong nutritional punch of peas and carrots, along with eggs for extra protein.

1 cup (140 g) frozen packaged mixed peas and carrots

1 medium head cauliflower, or half a head (2 cups/280 g riced) plus 2 cups cooked white rice (370 g) or cooked brown rice (390 g)

2 tablespoons sesame oil

1 or 2 garlic cloves, minced, or 1 to 3 teaspoons jarred minced garlic

2 large eggs, beaten

3 tablespoons soy sauce or tamari (gluten-free if needed)

1 Put the frozen peas and carrots on a plate, spreading them out to thaw slightly.

2 Break or chop the cauliflower, including the stem, into chunks about the size of a golf ball. Place these chunks in a food processor or blender and pulse until the pieces look like rice. (As an alternative method, teach your child how to use a box grater for this step: Wearing safety gloves, cut the cauliflower into four large pieces and grate them to create rice.)

3 Heat 1 tablespoon of the sesame oil in a large, deep skillet over medium-low heat. Add the riced cauliflower and garlic to the pan and stir slowly for 1 to 2 minutes, until the vegetables are barely starting to soften. Add the peas and carrots, rice (if using), and the remaining 1 tablespoon sesame oil and stir for 1 to 2 minutes to warm everything through.

④ Create a well in the center of the pan by pushing all of the mixture to the sides of the deep skillet. Pour the beaten eggs into the well, then cook, stirring continuously, until the scrambled eggs are at your preferred consistency. Turn off the heat.

⑤ Fold the eggs into the cauliflower mixture as you add the soy sauce. Serve warm.

All Kids Can . . .

- Spread the peas and carrots to thaw
- Wash and dry the cauliflower
- Chop the cauliflower with a kid-safe knife
- Put the cauliflower in the food processor and pulse (with an adult's help)
- Beat the eggs
- Hand ingredients to the chef as needed for cooking

Plus, Big Kids Can . . .

- Grate the cauliflower using safety gloves and adult supervision
- Cook the fried rice (with adult supervision)

PARENTING IN THE KITCHEN

Let your child take the lead about the possibility of adding other veggies to this dish. Got a slice of red bell pepper in your fridge? Encourage your child to dice it up and let him decide if he'd like to add it to the fried rice. Perhaps he would like to try adding a few slices of scallion or a few broccoli tops. It's worth mentioning again—keep it underwhelming so that kids feel confident in each step.

A Sweet Treat: Cauliflower Caramel Corn

TOTAL TIME: **40 minutes** PREP: **10 minutes** COOK: **30 minutes** SERVES: **4**

Use all the colors of cauliflower to make cauliflower "popcorn" sweetened with healthy coconut oil and just a dash of maple syrup. Stop by a dollar store or a party shop for red-and-white-striped popcorn bags to serve on family movie night!

4 large half heads cauliflower in 4 different colors
¼ cup (60 ml) melted coconut oil
2 tablespoons pure maple syrup
1 teaspoon ground cinnamon
Sea salt to taste

1 Preheat the oven to 400°F (200°C). Line two baking sheets with foil for easy cleanup.

2 Remove the core of the cauliflower (see instructions on page 215) and break off tiny florets (the size of popped popcorn) into a large bowl. (Cut off any extra stem pieces for making Cauliflower Fried Rice, page 222, another day.)

3 Combine the coconut oil, maple syrup, and cinnamon in a large bowl. Add the florets, coating evenly.

4 Spread the florets on the baking sheet, leaving space between the pieces for even browning. Roast for 30 minutes, or until the cauliflower is toasty brown on just the edges.

5 Remove from the oven, sprinkle with salt, and serve warm.

- Wash and dry the cauliflower
- Break tiny florets from the cauliflower head
- Combine the oil with the flavorings and toss in the florets
- Sprinkle the cooked florets with salt

KALE

Of course kale has vitamin K! Kale is splendid for bone and eye health, something all superheroes need! All of us have recollections of certain vegetables from our childhood. My friend Kristen Beddard has beloved memories of kale, something her mother told me she introduced to Kristen "at conception." Babies experience the tastes while floating in the amniotic fluid. Research has shown that when babies start eating solids, they demonstrate a preference for the vegetables their mothers ate during pregnancy. From nine months of age, Kristen's mom served it on a regular basis, in a variety of ways, just as we will by following the Three *E*'s. At twenty-nine, Kristen moved to Paris, only to discover that the French had no idea what kale was. Kristen single-handedly brought kale to a city that is famous for delicious food, convincing a world-famous Michelin star chef to use it in his recipes and farmers to plant it in the farms outside the city. She wrote about her quest in *Bonjour Kale: A Memoir of Paris, Love, and Recipes*. If she can do all that, we can convince our kids to eat it, too.

EXPOSE

Vegetable Bouquet Centerpiece

Boys and girls love making something special to display, especially when it can be placed on the mealtime table for all to see. This time of year is ideal for creating easy vegetable bouquets, with kale as the main attraction. If you've got several kids in your family, use small mason jars and create individual bouquets for each place setting, for a decorative touch that's also handy for nibbling—because kale is not only pretty, it's also just plain delicious.

What you'll need:

- Fresh kale leaves, ideally of two varieties (Try large leafy versions, like dinosaur kale or red Russian kale, as they tend to be less bitter and are quite pretty in arrangements.)
- Other raw vegetables such as cauliflower, carrots, and celery (optional)
- One large mason jar or vase (or smaller jars for individual bouquets)
- Flowers (optional)
- Stickers or other decorations for the jar (optional)

What to do:

1 KIDS: Wash any dirt from the vegetables and pat them dry. Fill a mason jar halfway with water. Add stickers or other decorations to the jar if you'd like.

2 PARENTS AND KIDS: Tear or cut leaves of kale and prep other vegetables that you want to add to your bouquet. For example, parents can peel carrots and slice them into long sticks to encourage sampling when making small bouquets! Leaves remaining on the celery sticks will add a lighter green color to the leafy mix of kale.

> ⌐ TIP ⌐
>
> You can store jars of kale and carrot and celery sticks in the refrigerator at night and they will last all week as a centerpiece for your table. Unless they get eaten, of course.

How your child benefits

Cooking is art, and art is a form of play. When kids first experience food with no expectations of eating it but instead use it to create something beautiful for all to admire, they like that food! Liking a new food doesn't always involve tasting. "I like to make bouquets of kale for my family" can quickly translate to "I like to make kale penne with my family" and eventually to "I like to make a big salad bar with my family." Start with one positive interaction and build the kale friendship from there.

Easy Cheesy Baked Kale Penne

TOTAL TIME: 3 hours PREP: 25 minutes COOK: 2½ hours
SERVES: 6 with leftovers

Slow cookers are great for overnight cooking, but I rarely remember to put something together before I go to bed. I'm more likely to panic midafternoon, asking, "What are we going to make for dinner?" No worries! This recipe cooks in just 2½ hours and can be assembled in a jiffy, with your kids' help. If you'd like to add a bit more flavor to this dish, try sprinkling adobo seasoning or Italian herb seasoning onto the cheesy top before serving. Both spice mixtures kick it up a notch!

Olive oil or nonstick cooking spray for greasing the slow cooker

2 pounds (905 g) lean ground beef, or 1 pound (455 g) lean ground beef plus 1 pound (455 g) Italian sausage

1½ cups (50 g) finely chopped kale leaves, stalks discarded (use a food processor or high-powered blender for chopping)

2 large eggs

One 15-ounce (425 g) container ricotta

½ cup (20 g) chopped fresh basil

1 cup (100 g) grated Asiago

1 cup (100 g) grated Parmesan

1 cup (100 g) plus ¼ cup (25 g) grated mozzarella

One 24-ounce (680 g) jar vodka sauce (or pasta sauce of your choice)

8 ounces (225 g) penne pasta (gluten-free if needed)

1 Grease the inside of a slow cooker with the oil.

2 Crumble and brown the beef in a pan on medium-high heat. (If you're using all lean beef, no draining should be necessary, but if you're using sausage, drain the fat.) Stir in the kale and remove the pan from the heat.

3 Whisk the eggs and combine them with the ricotta and basil. In a separate bowl, combine the Asiago, Parmesan, and 1 cup (100 g) of the mozzarella.

④ Spread one third of the pasta sauce in the bottom of the slow cooker and sprinkle a single layer of uncooked penne over the sauce. Sprinkle a third of the beef mixture over the penne. Using one third of the ricotta mixture, drop dollops of ricotta onto the beef. Sprinkle one third of the three-cheese mixture on top. Repeat the same pattern two more times. Add the remaining ¼ cup mozzarella on top of the last layer of cheese—because more cheese is always better.

⑤ Cover and cook on high for 2½ hours.

All Kids Can . . .

- Grease the inside of the slow cooker
- Put the kale in the food processor and pulse (with an adult's help)
- Whisk the eggs and combine them with the ricotta and basil
- Hand ingredients to the chef as needed while cooking
- Assemble the baked penne (with an adult's help)

Plus, Big Kids Can . . .

- Cook the beef (with adult supervision) (see safe meat handling instructions on page 113)
- Grate the cheeses using safety gloves (with adult supervision)

PARENTING IN THE KITCHEN

When introducing herbs to kids, a good placed to start is with fresh basil. The aroma is familiar if kids like pizza, and it's the most common herb used today, so it's the most familiar. It's amazing how many kids will bite into a leaf of basil but refuse to bite into any other leafy green. Encourage your child to chop the basil into tiny pieces, just like the small pieces of kale. When the baked penne is done, the two leafy greens are indistinguishable both in taste and appearance, because all of the flavors blend together in the slow cooker.

Kalitos

TOTAL TIME: **25 minutes** PREP: **15 minutes** COOK: **7 to 10 minutes** SERVES: **4**

When I first met Nimali Fernando—"Doctor Yum"—my coauthor for the book *Raising a Healthy, Happy Eater*, I proclaimed her "my pediatrician in the kitchen" because she has a huge teaching kitchen right in her pediatric office! In fact, she gives out more recipes than prescriptions. Doctor Yum introduced me to her recipe for "Veggitos" and we included it in our book. It was such a hit, I'm including the version for "Kalitos" here. Doctor Yum offers over one hundred recipes on her website, doctoryum.org, including how to use this same spice mix for squash, zucchini, jicama, and other veggies.

¼ cup (15 g) nutritional yeast
1 to 2 tablespoons sea salt
1 teaspoon chili powder
1 teaspoon ground cumin
1 teaspoon onion powder
1 teaspoon paprika
⅛ to ¼ teaspoon cayenne pepper (optional)
1 large bunch dinosaur kale or red Russian kale
2 tablespoons cooking oil of your choice (try coconut oil or avocado oil for a subtle difference in flavor)

① Preheat the oven to 350°F (180°C).

② Mix together the nutritional yeast, salt, chili powder, cumin, onion powder, paprika, and cayenne (if using). A great way to do the mixing is to pour everything into a jar, tighten the lid, and let your child shake, shake, shake!

③ Rinse the kale, remove the thick ribs from the leaves, and pat until very dry. Tear the leaves into bite-size pieces. Massage all sides of the kale with a very light layer of the oil. (You may have some oil left over.) Spread the kale pieces in a single layer on a baking sheet.

④ Bake for 7 to 10 minutes, until crispy, checking frequently toward the end of cooking to remove any chips that are getting crispy before the others and to ensure that none are burned. But it's the crispiness that gives kalito chips that satisfying crunch!

5 Remove the pan from the oven, sprinkle the seasoning over the kale, and gently toss.

All Kids Can . . .

- Mix the seasonings in a jar
- Rinse the kale, remove the thick rib from each leaf with a kid-safe knife, and pat dry
- Tear the kale leaves into bite-size pieces
- Massage the kale with oil
- Spread the kale on a baking sheet

PARENTING IN THE KITCHEN

Embrace your child's love for technology by introducing her to cooking sites that are designed to be inviting for kids. Doctor Yum's website (doctoryum.org) includes a unique and very cool feature called the Meal Maker Machine. You and your child can click on a list of ingredients that you already have on hand in the pantry or fridge and, presto, the Meal Maker Machine will instantly generate a recipe using those ingredients to help you create a curry, soup, stir-fry, salad, or other dish with instructions you can follow right from your computer screen.

Kale Salad Bar

TOTAL TIME: 20 to 30 minutes PREP: 20 to 30 minutes SERVES: 4 to 6

Don't let the term "salad" scare you away from this recipe. One of the easiest strategies for helping kids learn to love any salad is to deconstruct the final product by creating a salad bar. When kids participate in the food prep and arrange the salad bar for everyone to enjoy, they have a chance to nibble on ingredients and experience each one on its own. This experiential activity helps kids understand that separate ingredients mixed together doesn't create a foreign food. Instead they learn that they've created a yummy dish made up of foods they already love—like crunchy apple sticks.

KALE SALAD

2 tablespoons or more lemon juice, orange juice, or champagne vinegar

2 tablespoons or more honey, agave syrup, or pure maple syrup

2 tablespoons or more extra virgin olive oil or avocado oil (or other oil)

1 tablespoon Dijon mustard (optional)

Salt and black pepper to taste

1 bunch dinosaur kale or red Russian kale (or a combo of each), with ribs removed and leaves chopped into pieces the size of a pea (use a food processor or blender, or tear to your heart's content)

SALAD BAR

Set up an array with options in amounts that allow for 1 tablespoon of each choice per person. (Offer just a few options or a bunch, it's up to you!) Note: Asterisks indicate items that should be chopped small for kids under age three. And be sure that raisins or dried fruit do not bind together to form a choking hazard.

Nuts of your choice* (such as cashews, macadamias, or pecans)

Seeds of your choice* (such as raw or roasted sunflower or sprouted pumpkin seeds, but not for kids under three years old)

Raisins, currants, or chopped dried fruit of your choice*

Fresh fruit of your choice (pomegranate seeds, grapes*, chopped apples*, mango, or avocado)

Shredded or crumbled cheeses of your choice (Parmesan, cheddar, goat cheese, or blue cheese)

Vegetables of your choice* (finely chopped brussels sprouts, carrots, red cabbage, jicama*, or any other vegetables in this book!)

Proteins of your choice* (cooked chicken or beef, tofu, beans, or hard-boiled eggs—see Tip on quick-cooking meat, page 92 on brining and roasting chicken, and page 101 on cooking easy-to-peel eggs)

Whole wheat or gluten-free pasta, cooked and lightly coated with olive oil to prevent sticking

....

● To prepare the Kale Salad, whisk together the lemon juice, honey, oil, and mustard (if using) in a small bowl. Season with salt and pepper. Taste and add more lemon juice, oil, or honey if needed. The secret to a good dressing is taste testing and making it your own. Pour half of the dressing over the chopped kale in a large bowl and massage the kale with your hands. Add more if you like a wetter salad, but the leaves can soak up dressing and turn soggy over time, so be careful. By the time everyone has constructed their salad, the kale will be tender and sweet, just the way you like it!

❷ Serve the Kale Salad in bowls and let everyone add extra dressing and whatever toppings from the salad bar they like!

All Kids Can . . .

- Wash and dry the produce
- Chop the salad bar options with a kid-safe knife
- Whisk the dressing

- Add salt and pepper to the dressing and give it a taste test
- Assemble a beautiful salad bar!

 TIP

To add chicken or beef to a salad bar (or to other recipes in this book), this is the simplest method. Cut the meat into strips of equal thickness. Season with salt and pepper on both sides. Heat a skillet over medium-high heat. Add a thin coating of vegetable oil, allowing it to warm for a minute before placing each strip of meat in the pan. Cover and cook on low until cooked through, flipping over halfway through the cooking time (typically up to 5 minutes). Remove the meat from the heat immediately and allow it to rest for 5 minutes before slicing into smaller pieces for younger kids.

KITCHEN SCIENCE

Why massage kale? Kale is made of a fibrous structure called cellulose. All that fiber is soooo good for you, but it can also give you gas (shhh!) if you eat too much of it raw. By massaging the kale and using your hands to break up the cellulose while the acid seeps in to make the kale even softer, you've broken it down before digestion in your belly begins, reducing the likelihood it will create gas.

A Sweet Treat: Choco-Kale Frozen Pops

TOTAL TIME: **40 minutes** PREP: **10 minutes** SERVES: **4 to 6**

The combination of blueberries and cocoa powder is delicious and really great at hiding the color green. At this point in our kale adventure, kids have been exploring kale in multiple ways and they are active participants in adding kale to the rest of the ingredients. If they are still hesitant about eating the leafy greens, it helps their confidence to see it pulverized and then almost (but not quite!) disappear behind a curtain of chocolate-blueberry yumminess.

2 large kale leaves, washed and stems removed
1 cup (155 g) frozen blueberries
1 cup (280 g) vanilla 2 percent Greek yogurt
1 tablespoon unsweetened cocoa powder (preferably Guittard)
2 teaspoons honey, or more to taste
¼ cup (60 g) mini chocolate chips

1 Tear the kale leaves into several pieces and chop them finely in a food processor or blender.

2 Add the blueberries, yogurt, cocoa powder, and honey, blending until you see only very tiny specks of blueberry skin and kale. Stir in the mini chocolate chips, pour the mixture immediately into small ice pop molds, and freeze for at least 30 minutes. (Larger ice molds will take longer to freeze.)

All Kids Can . . .

• Rinse the kale and remove the thick rib with a kid-safe knife
• Tear the kale leaves
• Add the kale to a food processor or blender (with an adult's help)
• Add the other ingredients (with an adult's help)
• Stir in the mini chocolate chips
• Pour the mixture into ice pop molds (with an adult's help)

PARENTING IN THE KITCHEN

Adding texture to fun foods like ice pops is a terrific way to help your child adjust to small flecks of color in foods. They will see the specks of blueberry and kale, but the two are indistinguishable in taste when embedded in the frozen pop. The addition of mini chocolate chips adds to the texture, providing a bit of crunch with each bite.

PUMPKIN

Pumpkin improves digestion because it has a lot of fiber, but its bright orange color tells us that it's also loaded with vitamin A. If you've got little kids, you've probably made a jack-o'-lantern with a large pumpkin purchased at a pumpkin patch or local market. Smaller baking pumpkins, sometimes called sugar pumpkins or pie pumpkins, are 6 to 8 inches (15 to 20 cm) in diameter and the best choice for the following activities and recipes. One pumpkin this size yields about 15 ounces (425 g) of pumpkin puree, the same amount typically sold in cans. Baking pumpkins have flesh that is delicious when roasted, pureed, or added to soups or pies but are seasonal and rarely found in stores past fall. Canned pumpkin is wonderful, too; just be sure to read the label to make sure it's 100 percent pumpkin puree and not pumpkin pie filling with added sugar.

EXPOSE

Pumpkin Bowl Toss

Half the fun of this game is creating the pumpkin bowls, which can be used for serving soup (see Tip) when the game is over! Some people are sensitive to pumpkin on their skin—consider wearing rubber gloves when cleaning out the pumpkins.

What you'll need:

- 4 or 5 small baking pumpkins (also called pie pumpkins or sugar pumpkins)
- Paring knife
- Sturdy metal spoons for scooping out seeds and stringy fibers

- 8 to 12 heavy baby carrots, broccoli stems, or other heavy veggies for each player
- 4 or 5 dry washcloths

What to do:

1 **KIDS:** Wash and dry the pumpkins.

2 **PARENTS:** Use a paring knife to cut a large circle around the stem of each pumpkin. Remove the "lid."

3 **PARENTS AND KIDS:** Scoop out the stringy fibers from the inside of the pumpkin and discard, but save the seeds; see the Tip on how to roast them! Position the pumpkin bowls at different distances on clean washcloths on the floor. Try to toss the baby carrots or broccoli stems into the bowls. The farther away the bowl, the more points for getting a veggie in the bowl.

Can you toss from your knees, on tiptoe, or behind your back?

>**TIP**<

Roasting pumpkin seeds is fun, and they make a yummy snack, but seeds should not be served to kids under the age of three. To make roasted pumpkin seeds, preheat the oven to 300°F (150°C). Wipe any fiber off the seeds. Toss the seeds in a bowl with a little melted unsalted butter and salt. Spread the seeds in a single layer on a baking sheet and bake for about 45 minutes, stirring occasionally, until golden brown. If you'd like to save the bowls for the pumpkin bisque recipe ahead, rinse them out and pat them dry. Cover them in foil, refrigerate, and bake within two days for with the bisque recipe on page 242.

How your child benefits

Not only are kids learning about all aspects of pumpkins (seeds, rind, flesh) in this activity, but they are also developing their coordination and the ability to adjust the amount of force in order to find the target. Most importantly, the pumpkin bowl toss teaches kids to keep trying. If you've ever been to a carnival and tried to toss a ball into a bucket from a distance, you know it's not easy! This game teaches kids to be persistent and have fun in the process of learning a new skill.

Power-Packed Pumpkin Snacks

TOTAL TIME: 40 minutes PREP: 10 minutes BAKE: 30 minutes MAKES: 24 small cookies

Chopped pumpkin seeds, almond flour, and pumpkin puree join forces to create power-packed snacks that kids can't get enough of. Although this recipe uses muffin pans with paper liners, these snacks are more like a light, soft cookie nestled in paper. They don't rise the way muffins do, because they have less sugar—but the pumpkin seed crumble on top adds a lovely hint of sweetness. Get ready for a little package of autumn, with a hint of fall spices.

Nonstick cooking spray

2 cups (220 g) almond flour

2 teaspoons baking powder (gluten-free if needed)

1 tablespoon pumpkin pie spice

½ teaspoon salt

1 cup (200 g) plus 1 tablespoon packed light brown sugar

6 tablespoons (85 g) unsalted butter, at room temperature

3 large eggs

1⅓ cups (320 g) pumpkin puree (if you'd like to make your own and don't plan to save the pumpkin bowls for the Pumpkin Bisque, see Tip)

1 teaspoon pure vanilla extract

⅓ cup (45 g) raw, sprouted or fresh unshelled pumpkin seeds (for kids under three years old, chop the seeds)

1 Preheat the oven to 350°F (180°C). Line two 12-cup muffin pans with paper liners. Spray each liner with cooking spray.

2 In a medium bowl, whisk together the flour, baking powder, spice, and salt.

3 In a large bowl, use an electric mixer to cream together 1 cup (200 g) of the sugar and the butter until the mixture is light and fluffy. Beat in the eggs, one at a time. Fold in the pumpkin puree and vanilla extract. Fold in the flour mixture. Be gentle—don't overmix!

4 Mix the pumpkin seeds and the remaining 1 tablespoon sugar in a small bowl.

⑤ Fill each cupcake liner halfway with batter. Sprinkle the top of each cup with the seed mixture.

⑥ Bake for 30 minutes, or until a toothpick inserted in the center of a cookie comes out clean.

All Kids Can . . .

- Chop the pumpkin seeds (if necessary) with a kid-safe knife
- Line the muffin pans with liners
- Whisk the dry ingredients
- Cream the sugar and butter (with an adult's help)
- Beat in the eggs (with an adult's help)
- Fold in the other ingredients
- Mix the seeds and sugar for topping
- Fill the liners (use a small scoop for easy filling)

TIP

To make pumpkin puree from fresh pumpkins, preheat the oven to 350°F (175°C). Use two of the pumpkin bowls from the Pumpkin Bowl Toss (page 238) if you don't plan to save them for Pumpkin Bisque (page 242) and cut each in half. Place the halves face up on two baking sheets and roast for about 45 minutes, until the pumpkin is fork tender and golden brown. Remove the pumpkin halves from the pan and let cool slightly before peeling away the outer skin. Cut into chunks and put the chunks into a food processor. Pulse until smooth, adding a tablespoon of water at a time during the pulsing if it looks too dry. Use immediately or freeze in a plastic freezer bag, pushing out all the air before sealing. The pumpkin will retain its full flavor for up to six months.

Pumpkin Bisque with Crispy Sage Leaves

TOTAL TIME: 35 minutes (not including pumpkin bowls) **PREP:** 20 minutes **COOK:** 15 minutes
SERVES: 4 or 5 with leftovers

Get fancy and serve this bisque in small edible pumpkin bowls if you made them for the Pumpkin Bowl Toss (page 238). But whatever you do, don't skip the crispy sage leaves! Sage takes on a different flavor when fried to a delicate crisp in butter or oil. Although the sage is used as a lovely garnish in this recipe, you might want to fry up a few extra leaves to snack on while setting the table.

4 or 5 small baking (pie or sugar) pumpkins (optional)
4 tablespoons olive oil
½ onion, chopped
2 garlic cloves, minced
One 13.5-ounce (398 ml) can coconut milk
1 cup (240 g) pumpkin puree (see Tip on page 241 to make it from the pumpkin bowls, if you are not using them for serving, or from 2 other pumpkins)
1 cup (240 ml) chicken or vegetable broth, or more if you prefer a milder soup
½ teaspoon ground cumin
¼ teaspoon ground cardamom
¼ teaspoon ground nutmeg
⅛ teaspoon ground cinnamon
Pinch of paprika (optional)
Pinch of cayenne pepper (optional)
Sea salt and black pepper to taste
10 to 12 fresh sage leaves, rinsed and thoroughly patted dry

1 To make the pumpkin bowls (if using), preheat the oven to 350°F (180°C). Scoop out the seeds following the instructions on page 239, reserving them for toasting, if desired (see Tip on page 239). Place the pumpkins in a large shallow roasting pan. Cover with foil and bake for 30 to 45 minutes, until tender but still holding their shape.

2 In a 4-quart (3.8 L) round casserole or similar deep pot, heat 1 tablespoon of the oil over medium heat and sauté the onion until soft and fragrant. Add the garlic and sauté for 1 minute. Add the coconut milk, pumpkin puree, broth, cumin, cardamom, nutmeg, cinnamon, paprika (if using), cayenne (if using), salt, and pepper. Whisk the soup together and cook until warmed through.

3 While the soup is warming, heat the remaining 3 tablespoons oil over medium-high heat in a small saucepan. Carefully place a few sage leaves at a time into the oil, frying them for a few minutes on each side until the edges are slightly brown. Remove the leaves with a slotted spoon and drain on paper towels. Sprinkle them with salt while they're still warm.

4 Serve the soup in bowls with a few crumbled sage leaves on top for garnish.

All Kids Can . . .

- Help make the pumpkin bowls (if using)
- Garnish the soup with crumbled sage leaves

Plus, Big Kids Can . . .

- Chop the onion with a sharp knife (with adult supervision)
- Add ingredients to the soup (with adult supervision)

KITCHEN SCIENCE

Vegetable or fruit? Shhh . . . pumpkins are one of those vegetables that aren't really vegetables. Horticulturally speaking, they are a fruit—and technically a berry. Without going into a lot of botanical mumbo-jumbo, suffice it to say that this distinction has to do with the way a pumpkin grows from a single flower on a vine. Cucumbers and tomatoes are also berries. Berry, berry interesting, is it not?

Speedy, Sweet, and Spicy Pumpkin Chili

TOTAL TIME: 45 minutes (not including chicken or squash prep) PREP: 25 minutes
COOK: 20 minutes SERVES: 6 with leftovers

The combination of textures in chili can be a stretch for kids, but half the fun of this meal is making it and tasting each ingredient, one at a time. This chili is speedy to assemble and offers a wonderful range of flavors for tiny tasters! What's more, it freezes well, so you can easily store some for future meals and allow kids to get exposure to the same tastes and textures over time. Top this satisfying dish with sour cream, shredded cheese, crushed corn chips, sliced shallots, sliced scallions, or any other possibilities you have on hand. Leave out the meat and opt for vegetable broth if you prefer a vegetarian chili.

1 tablespoon olive oil

1 medium onion, chopped

4 garlic cloves, minced

1 tablespoon chili powder

1 tablespoon ground cumin

1 teaspoon dried oregano

½ teaspoon smoked paprika

1 pound (455 g) ground turkey, lean ground beef, or shredded cooked chicken (see Tips on pages 92 and 235 on cooking chicken)

One 28-ounce (794 g) diced fire-roasted tomatoes (with juices)

One 15.5-ounce (439 g) can black beans (drained and rinsed)

One 15.5-ounce (439 g) can red kidney beans (drained and rinsed)

1¾ cups or one 15-ounce can (425 g) pumpkin puree

1½ cups (360 ml) chicken or vegetable broth, plus more if needed

1⅓ cups (340 g) salsa verde (from a jar is fine)

3 tablespoons light brown sugar

1 tablespoon ground cinnamon

1 teaspoon ground nutmeg

1 teaspoon salt

1 teaspoon black pepper

2 cups (200 g) cubed butternut squash or pumpkin, roasted following directions on page 28 (optional)

2 cups (60 g) fresh spinach leaves (optional)

❶ Heat the oil in a large pot over medium-high heat. Add the onion and cook for about 5 minutes, until translucent. Add the garlic and cook for 1 minute more. Add the chili powder, cumin, oregano, and paprika, and stir to combine.

❷ If you're using ground turkey or beef, crumble and add it to the chili now, cooking thoroughly for about 5 minutes, until there is no pink in the center, and making sure there are no large chunks.

❸ Stir in the tomatoes, beans, pumpkin puree, broth, salsa, sugar, cinnamon, nutmeg, salt, and pepper.

❹ If you're using shredded cooked chicken, stir that in now and let it simmer in the chili until ready to serve.

❺ Stir in the squash and spinach (if using). Serve immediately.

All Kids Can . . .

- Shred the cooked chicken (if using)
- Drain and rinse the beans
- Hand ingredients to the chef while cooking
- Taste-test—blow on samples first!

Plus, Big Kids Can . . .

- Cook the entire recipe (with adult supervision)!

PARENTING IN THE KITCHEN

Many of the recipes in this book instruct cooks to add spices according to taste. Encouraging your child to taste as he cooks develops a more sophisticated palate, but it also alleviates the hesitancy that many children have to trying new foods. As we've said before, when we do a taste test, we aren't expecting it to be delicious yet. The purpose is to determine what else it needs . . . More cinnamon? A bit more brown sugar? Giving your child some control over what to add to each dish builds confidence in the kitchen.

A Sweet Treat: Petite Pumpkin Pies

TOTAL TIME: **45 minutes plus 1 hour to chill the dough** PREP: **20 minutes** COOK: **25 minutes**
MAKES: **24 mini pies**

Pumpkin pie is one of the easiest desserts to make, but a typical slice of pie is too big for little bellies, and traditional recipes can contain lots of sugar. Try these petite versions instead, using unsweetened coconut milk. Kids adore making these because they get to mold the piecrust into tiny cups and fill each one with a tablespoon of pumpkin. Save a few for a little lunchbox love the next day, so the kids can show their friends what they made.

- 1¼ cups (155 g) all-purpose flour (reduce amount to 1 cup/140 g if using gluten-free all-purpose flour), plus more for your hands
- ½ teaspoon coarse salt
- 1 stick (½ cup/115 g) unsalted butter, chilled and cut into 1-inch (2.5 cm) pieces
- 2 to 4 tablespoons ice water
- 2 medium eggs (3 if using gluten-free flour)
- Nonstick cooking spray
- 1 cup (240 g) pumpkin puree
- ½ cup to ⅔ cup (115 to 140 g) coconut cream from a can of coconut milk (see Tip)
- ⅓ cup (65 g) sugar
- 1 teaspoon ground cinnamon
- ½ teaspoon ground cloves
- ½ teaspoon ground nutmeg
- ¼ teaspoon allspice
- ¼ teaspoon ground ginger
- Homemade Whipped Cream (page 68) for topping (optional)

1. In a food processor, pulse the flour and salt to combine. Add the pieces of butter down the chute, pulsing until the mixture resembles fine meal. Add 2 tablespoons of the ice water (plus 1 egg if using gluten-free flour) and pulse until well combined, about

1 minute. The resulting dough should hold together, but it may need a bit more water if it seems too dry. At this point you can wrap the dough in plastic wrap and refrigerate it for 1 hour for easier handling—but most kids can't wait to start making the pie cups!

2 Preheat the oven to 375°F (190°C). Spray a 24-hole mini-muffin pan with nonstick cooking spray.

3 Drop 1 teaspoon of dough into each cup in the muffin pan. Tap your fingers into some flour and push down the center of the dough, then mold the dough up the sides of the cup, doing your best to keep even pressure to create the mini piecrusts. The edges should just reach the top of the cup.

4 Whisk together the pumpkin puree, coconut cream, sugar, cinnamon, cloves, nutmeg, allspice, and ginger. Taste-test and consider adding a pinch more of any of your favorite spices. Whisk in the 2 eggs, but do not overwhisk.

5 Drop about 1 tablespoon of the filling into each piecrust. Bake for 25 minutes, or until a toothpick inserted in the center of one of the pies comes out clean.

6 Cool slightly to allow the filling to set before removing the pies from the pan.

7 Top with whipped cream, if desired.

All Kids Can . . .

- Add dough ingredients to the food processor and pulse (with adult supervision)
- Spray the muffin pan
- Create the mini crusts
- Whisk the filling
- Add the filling to the crusts
- Top with whipped cream (if using)

TIP

Most cans of coconut milk that have been sitting undisturbed on a pantry shelf for a while will have separated into a watery, clear liquid and a thicker coconut cream. But if you want to be sure the contents will be well separated when you go to use the milk, put the can in the fridge overnight before opening it. Spoon off the cream, and save the watery liquid—stored in a sealed container, it will last for a few days in the refrigerator, available to use for soups or curries.

ACKNOWLEDGMENTS

My heartfelt thanks—

To the publishing team at The Experiment, whose positive feedback kept me on track to create a book that brings parents and kids back to the heart of the home: the kitchen. I am so grateful for the support of Matthew Lore, Batya Rosenblum, Jeanne Tao, Joan Strasbaugh, Sarah Smith, and Jennifer Hergenroeder, who offered expert guidance throughout this journey and always with a smile. It has been my honor to have two books published by The Experiment, and I'm thankful for the team's experience and sense of humor in what can be a very tedious yet glorious process!

To the numerous professionals who join me in the quest to make family mealtimes a priority in every household. You inspire me every day.

To the families I treat in feeding therapy on a weekly basis. Thank you for welcoming me into your homes, knowing that this won't be easy and will take time. It's always one of the most rewarding moments of my life to see your child progress from a hesitant eater to a learning eater to an adventurous little foodie, and I am honored to be a part of your food adventure.

And finally, with the most loving gratitude, to my husband, Bob, and my precious daughters, Mallory and Carly. Thank you for rooting me on, tasting new recipes, and giving me your honest opinions, even when I grumbled at having to start over again. Your love and support mean everything to me, and always will.

APPENDIX 1
Addressing Feeding and Sensory Challenges

FOR A SURPRISING NUMBER OF children, even if parents are following the Three *E*'s, learning to eat a variety of foods can be challenging. A range of research suggests that as many as 25 to 45 percent of typically developing children demonstrate feeding challenges. The prevalence is even higher for children with developmental disorders.[1] If you feel concerned about your child's ability to enjoy a variety of foods or if you observe any of the red flags from the list below, ask your child's pediatrician to refer your child for a feeding evaluation:[2]

Concerns About Toddlers

Feeding my toddler is frustrating. Perhaps she spits out her food and just wants milk, or she throws her plate or cup. There are many reasons that kids behave the way they do, but a trained pediatric professional who specializes in all aspects of feeding skills can help you determine *why* your child is behaving this way and what to do about it.

My toddler hasn't grown much and my pediatrician is concerned. He hasn't yet been diagnosed with "failure to thrive," but your instincts tell you it's time to seek help. Failure to thrive is a specific medical diagnosis with criteria on how much a child has stalled in growth. But many pediatricians wisely refer kids who are not taking in adequate calories to feeding therapy *before* those criteria have been met.

My toddler refuses to eat anything but his favorites. Toddlers often go on "food jags," where they insist on eating the same foods, over and over. Problem is, they eventually get tired of eating the same thing and the list of preferred foods begins to dwindle. A feeding evaluation will tell you two things—first, whether your child is exhibiting typical, age-appropriate picky eating and, second, how to prevent this particular stage in toddler life from becoming a problem in the near future.

My toddler eats great at school, but not at home. Feeding therapy, especially when the evaluation and treatment are conducted in the home, can pinpoint why a toddler is a more hesitant eater at home than in other environments. Another example of context-dependent picky eating is the child who cannot tolerate eating in restaurants. Many times a restaurant is too stimulating for a child's sensory systems.

Concerns About Preschool and School-Age Children

His siblings label him "the picky eater of the family." Kids will most often live up to the labels we assign to them: "Oh, he's our math whiz" or "She's our little athlete" or "He's our picky eater." A feeding therapist can help "your picky eater" begin to think of himself differently.

My child has food allergies. One of the challenges that parents encounter when their child has food allergies is figuring out what to offer and how to expand a child's food preferences while keeping them safe. Be sure the therapist you choose has extensive experience with children with food allergies and food intolerances.

My kid cannot eat in the school cafeteria. Feeding therapists are often welcomed into schools to provide strategies for both the child and the staff, so kids can eat a relaxed lunch with their friends and get some important nutrition before academics start that afternoon.

My kid wants to eat the same food as his friends, but he never learned to like that food. This situation is more common than you might expect. Kids who eat only chicken nuggets or macaroni and cheese limit themselves when the other students at school are hanging out at restaurants and food-centered events.

Whatever the reason, whatever the age, there is support for your child and your family, and stress-free mealtimes are possible. If you have just *one* meal per day together, in the course of childhood that daily meal will equate to over six thousand meals you'll be sharing. Focus on family and get there by parenting in the kitchen. If you need an extra guide on this journey, a feeding therapist is just one of the professionals who can help.

Throughout *Adventures in Veggieland*, I've pointed out the importance of exploring food with all of our senses. For children who have disorganized sensory systems or ones who overreact or underreact to certain stimuli, food exploration may seem quite challenging. But with a few slight adaptations in the kitchen, these "sensory kids" will benefit from connecting with you in the kitchen. In my article "The Cooking Connection,"[3] I offer the following strategies for parents:

To begin the process of introducing a child with sensory challenges to cooking, consider what skills are already in place. Develop strategies to build upon those existing skills and then branch out to more challenging activities. Break each recipe into stages, encouraging kids to participate wherever they can:

- **Stage one.** Assemble all equipment, utensils, or therapy tools for the recipe.

- **Stage two.** Assemble all foods, measuring and pouring ingredients into individual bowls. (Professional chefs call this *mise en place*, meaning "everything in its place.")

- **Stage three.** Following the recipe, assign specific tasks to the child, such as stirring or pouring. Teach tasks as needed, breaking each one into tiny steps. For example, one of my clients did not have the attention span (yet) for mixing dough but enjoyed lining up the spices according to color and handing them to me as I called out the name and color of the spice: "Green oregano! Black pepper!"

- **Stage four.** Clean up. Rinsing and loading a dishwasher is part of the cooking process. No dishwasher? A bucket of soapy water and a bucket of clean water plus a few towels will do the trick. Break down the sequence of scraping, washing, and rinsing (or loading the dishwasher) into smaller steps for a child who needs that—or with more than one kid, help them work on sequencing the steps together.

Kids with sensory difficulties may find the kitchen to be overwhelming at first. In "The Cooking Connection," I explore how each child has a distinct sensory system that may require various adaptations to make the kitchen a more welcoming environment.

Experiencing Food Through Sense

Seeing and Experiencing Food

From birth, humans use vision in conjunction with the other senses to make sense of their surroundings. As we grow, we log and categorize visual input in our brains to compare this input to new experiences and environments. For the child with sensory difficulties, past experiences with food will determine how easily she will adjust to new experiences. The kitchen environment is a unique part of the home, often filled with visual input like blinking lights, digital timers on microwaves or stoves, unusual blinds, overhead fluorescent light sources, and other stimuli. Stand back and take a long look at the kitchen before inviting a hesitant participant into the cooking environment. Is there anything that needs to be adjusted, softened, or moved, in order to make the kitchen more welcoming? Consider visual cues to help a child adapt to routines, such as a visual schedule of pictures that illustrates six steps to hand washing before handling food: (1) Turn water on. (2) Soap hands. (3) Rub hands together. (4) Rinse. (5) Turn water off. (6) Dry hands. Starting every cooking session with a familiar routine, like hand washing, is comforting to children, especially those with highly disorganized sensory systems, because they need an element of "sameness" or familiarity before encountering new experiences.

When kids are first learning to tolerate the visual input of the kitchen, consider the visual input of the food as well. Part of the cooking process will involve tasting as we cook. Professional chefs use tiny tasting spoons to dip and taste, then they season and grab a new spoon to repeat the process until the food is to their liking. Keep a small cup of tiny tasting spoons within easy reach as you cook together. A child is more likely to taste elements of the recipe using the tip of a small spoon that he can immediately throw into a wash bin, because it's quick and he can control how much he'll put on the spoon. But this tasting is also a visual activity: You'll be modeling "tiny tastes" frequently throughout your time together in the kitchen. As your child observes you sampling the foods, you'll be helping her build a relationship with a new food via positive visual input. So be sure to smile if it tastes good! And if the food is not quite to your liking (or your child's), model how to improve the taste by adding other ingredients, such as seasonings, and taste again. One of the most important aspects in helping any child become more adventurous with food is teaching her to be comfortable with tiny tastes, even if she communicates that she doesn't like that food. Learning to taste-test a nonpreferred food in order to change it just slightly and make it suit a particular palate is the essence of both good cooking and good feeding therapy. Every sample of food may not taste good, but we still need to taste it so we can decide how to change it from yucky to yummy. When kids say to me, "I don't want to taste it, I won't like it!" I always respond "Sweetheart, it's OK not to like it, we are just testing it." Remember, it's not always love at first sight. Sometimes a relationship with a new food takes time.

Listening and Experiencing Food

Some people are auditory learners, some visual, and some kinesthetic. Whatever their learning style, kids will often be sensitive to auditory stimuli. Sounds echoing on the hard surfaces of the kitchen can be a special challenge. Countertops, appliances, and tile or wood floors cause the sounds of electric appliances to reverberate onto highly sensitive eardrums. Just the tin-like sound of a whisk in a cold metal bowl working its magic as it whips liquid into solid whipped cream can be incredibly uncomfortable for a child with auditory hypersensitivities. When you're using blenders, food processors, or other large motorized appliances, pull the appliance away from the wall. Place the base of the appliance on a folded kitchen towel to absorb some of the vibration. A small towel placed over the top of the appliance and parted like a curtain helps quiet the sound from the machine while still allowing for ventilation and providing a small window to watch food be processed or blended. A set of headphones kept in the kitchen for the moment the appliances are turned on can add an extra level of comfort. Playing favorite music in the background or through headphones can also help regulate sensory systems and refocus the brain on more pleasing auditory stimuli.

Background sounds in the environment have been shown to influence our interpretation of taste, changing our perception of sweet to slightly bitter and causing other adjustments in our taste sensations, according to researchers including Charles Spence of the Crossmodal Research Laboratory at Oxford University.[4] This ongoing work may unearth how certain sounds in our environment could be manipulated to support those with highly sensitive taste buds or those who are hypersensitive to auditory input. Raise your own awareness of background sounds by closing your eyes and being still while standing in the kitchen. Listen to kitchen sounds that you may have been filtering out, like the fan above the stove, the quiet hum of the dishwasher, or the drip, drip, drip of the coffee maker as it brews. Be conscious of subtle background noise that may be distracting or may otherwise alter a child's perceptions in the kitchen.

Experiencing Food via Touch

The kitchen is an environment full of various surfaces, objects, and foods that can provide both pleasant and unpleasant tactile sensation to the skin even before children are exposed to the tactile element of tasting. Kids with tactile sensitivity may be more reserved about interacting in the kitchen if they find the room's tactile input upsetting. Consider the following:

1. Would this child feel more comfortable with soft cloth towels or stiffer paper towels?

2. Would this child have easy access to the sink to wash hands immediately if she needed to, in order to provide relief from messy hands or from a surface that is just too challenging for her to encounter? One of my clients was cautious to rest his hands or forearms on a chilly granite countertop, but he gradually became accustomed to it when he was invited to move his arms occasionally under warm running water.

3. Which spoon would be best suited for this child—a longer or shorter handle? For kids with tactile sensitivity, a longer-handled spoon may provide just enough distance from the texture of the food to allow her to interact in a comfortable manner with the spoon. Eventually, therapists want the child to feel at ease with touching the food and even using their hands to stir it; and gradually offering a shorter and shorter handle brings the child's hand closer to the food slowly over time.

The Sense of Balance in Food Exploration

While trying to help a child eat a more balanced diet, keep in mind that the child's physical sense of balance comes into play, too! Our awareness of balance and movement, detected in the inner ear and known as the vestibular system, is the foundation for all motor skills, both gross and fine. Biting, chewing, and swallowing are fine motor skills—involving the small muscles of the face and mouth—and every child needs a sense of being grounded, feeling adequate balance and stability, in their world in order to practice those skills. Imagine tasting new foods at the kitchen counter while standing on one foot. What a challenging and slightly unsettling experience! For kids who have poor vestibular processing, standing still in the kitchen can be tough. Many kids need to move in order to pay attention and regulate their body. The vestibular system works closely with our sense of proprioception (described below) so that we can adjust our movements to cut an apple, stab a pea with our fork, or step onto a step stool to reach the counter without injury.

Body Awareness and Food
Proprioception refers to the child's awareness of where various body parts are in space while considering how much effort must be used to move each part in a coordinated and effective manner. We use this sense quite often in the kitchen—when we fold almost weightless chocolate chips into thick, heavy cookie dough, reach carefully for something across a crowded countertop, or move about the kitchen without banging into open cabinet doors.

Various activities in the kitchen are dependent on the vestibular and proprioceptive receptors in the body and can be useful in calming and organizing a child. Activities such as stirring thick dough, carrying heavy cookbooks to the counter, and rolling out pizza dough with a rolling pin all have an integral centering effect. If possible, provide opportunities for kids to move about the kitchen periodically so that they are not standing in one place for too long.

Smelling and Experiencing Food
In our book *Raising a Healthy, Happy Eater*, Nimali Fernando and I explain the emotional connection between food exploration and the sense of smell:

> If you could peer into the human brain, the physical link between smell, emotion, and memory would be clear to see. The olfactory nerve is near the amygdala, the emotional center of the brain, and the hippocampus, the brain's memory center. For young children exploring new foods, just one unpleasant olfactory experience—the sulfur-like smell of rotten hard-boiled eggs, for example—can influence future interactions with that same food.[5]

Now consider that the child with sensory difficulties may have an olfactory system that is hypo- or hypersensitive. When the scents in the kitchen are more than a child can tolerate, consider the following strategies: (1) Allow the child to hold a small soft cloth with a preferred smell to hold up to her nose occasionally when new aromas become overwhelming. (2) Sip water through a small straw to filter out aromas. (3) Chew a fresh piece of gum to mask any unpleasant aromas.

Tasting and Experiencing Food

If aromas are not easily apparent to a child because of a hyposensitive olfactory system, she will rely mainly on the sense of taste when sampling new foods. In the inside of our noses, we have millions of receptor cells that detect odors. The receptor cells on our tongue detect five different tastes: salty, sweet, bitter, sour, and umami. As we taste foods, the air that is circulating in our mouths carries those aromas to the olfactory receptors—and the brain registers that taste plus the smell. That combination, taste plus smell, equals flavor. When kids have limited input via the olfactory nerve, they have difficulty detecting flavors. They may prefer stronger input via taste receptors to take in the full experience or to detect differences among foods.

The sense of taste is not only enhanced by the sense of smell but also by thousands of nerve endings that detect certain qualities of food. Consider the sensation of cool mint on your tongue versus the warmth of a spice like cinnamon. For many children, this interplay is best approached by introducing aromas before taste. Try using spice jars that allow for a smaller whiff of the scent. Many come with adjustable caps that allow for just a few holes to be exposed, but a simple piece of tape over most of the holes does the trick! A child may approach a new taste with caution, too. One set of researchers has suggested that approximately 25 percent of people are "super-tasters" who taste more intensely and 25 percent are "non-tasters." The rest of the population falls in the middle of the spectrum, with 50 percent happily tasting foods without hypo- or hypersensitive tongues.[6] Other research indicates that super-tasters have an extreme olfactory experience, too.[7] When trying new tastes with a hesitant eater, remember to (1) keep samples small, (2) deconstruct more complicated flavors into individual components first, and (3) consider texture, temperature, and other sensory components of each individual food.

APPENDIX 2
Resources and Suggested Products

Professional Resources

The following professionals contributed recipes or advice for this book. Visit their websites for more resources to help you raise adventurous eaters!

Clancy Cash Harrison, MS, RDN, FAND
fieldsofflavor.com

Laura Fuentes
momables.com

Jill Castle, MS, RDN, CDN
jillcastle.com

Chase Bailey
chasenyurface.com

Judy Delaware, OTR/L
feedinglittles.com

Ben Chansingthong
urbanthaicafe.com

Nimali Fernando (Dr. Yum), MD, MPH
doctoryum.org

Mia McCloy, OTR/L
boulderkidspot.com

Sarah Vance, nutritionist
rebalancelife.com

Products

The following companies make my favorite products for connecting with kids in the kitchen and at mealtimes!

Blendtec high-powered blenders
This is my favorite brand of high-powered blender, because it can often take the place of a food processor for recipes such as Parsnip-Carrot Mac 'n' Cheese.
blendtec.com

Bob's Red Mill Gluten-Free

Bob's Red Mill offers gluten-free flours, baking mixes, seeds, grains, and other products, and their blog includes gluten-free recipes.

bobsredmill.com

Chef'n Looseleaf Kale and Greens Stripper and FreshForce Garlic Press

The leaf stripper has different-sized holes for pulling stems through to remove the leaves, and the garlic press creates minced garlic with little effort.

chefn.com

Ezpz Happy Mat, Happy Bowl, and Flower Play Mat

These bowls and plates with built-in placemats stick to the counter when cooking.

ezpzfun.com

FunBites

Kid-safe food cutters can be used to create fun shapes.

funbites.com

Fun Eating Devices (FED) Sporkman, Gator Grips, and Crabby Grabby

Sporkman is a spork and chopsticks all in one, while Gator Grips and Crabby Grabby are like pull-action tongs!

funwithfed.com

Kuhn Rikon Kinderkitchen Dog Knives and Duck Snippers

Kid-safe knives and shears with rounded tips and blades are sharp enough to cut food but not fingers.

us.kuhnrikon.com

Microplane Cut-Resistant Glove

Cut-resistant fibers keep hands safe while using sharp blades.

microplaneintl.com

Orgain Kids Protein

These yummy organic protein shakes with non-GMO blended veggies support your child's journey to veggie love, with no corn syrup, no preservatives, and nothing artificial.

orgain.com/products/healthy-kids-organic-nutritional-shakes

OXO Good Grips Splatter Screen

A perforated stainless steel screen keeps hot oil from splattering onto surfaces, including skin.

oxo.com

NOTES

Introduction

1 CDC Vital Signs, "Progress on Children Eating More Fruit, Not Vegetables," Centers for Disease Control and Prevention website, August 2014, cdc.gov/vitalsigns/fruit-vegetables.

2 Shanthy A. Bowman, Steven L. Gortmaker, Cara B. Ebbeling, Mark A. Pereira, and David S. Ludwig, "Effects of Fast-Food Consumption on Energy Intake and Diet Quality Among Children in a National Household Survey," *Pediatrics* 113, no. 1 (January 2004), pediatrics .aappublications.org/content/113/1/112?download=true.

3 Ibid.

4 Kelly M. Purtell and Elizabeth T. Gershoff, "Fast Food Consumption and Academic Growth in Late Childhood," *Clinical Pediatrics* 54, no. 9 (2015), journals.sagepub.com/doi/ abs/10.1177/0009922814561742.

5 Allison Aubrey, "About a Third of US Kids and Teens Ate Fast Food Today," *NPR: All Things Considered*, September 17, 2015, npr.org/sections/thesalt/2015/09/17/440951329/about-a-third-of-u-s-kids-and-teens-ate-fast-food-today.

6 Betty Ruth Carruth, Paula J. Ziegler, Anne Gordon, and Susan I. Barr, "Prevalence of Picky Eaters Among Infants and Toddlers and Their Caregivers' Decisions About Offering a New Food," *Journal of the American Dietetic Association* 104 (January 2004): 57–64.

7 Paul Dazeley and Carmel Houston-Price, "Exposure to Foods' Non-Taste Sensory Properties: A Nursery Intervention to Increase Children's Willingness to Try Fruit and Vegetables," *Appetite* 84 (January 1, 2015): 1–6.

8 Chantal Nederkoorn, Anita Jansen, and Remco C. Havermans, "Feel Your Food: The Influence of Tactile Sensitivity on Picky Eating in Children," *Appetite* 84 (January 2015): 7–10.

9 Paul Dazeley, Carmel Houston-Price, and Claire Hill, "Should Healthy Eating Programmes Incorporate Interaction with Foods in Different Sensory Modalities? A Review of the Evidence," *British Journal of Nutrition* 108, no. 5 (January 2012): 769–77.

10 Carmel Houston-Price, Laurie Butler, and Paula Shiba, "Visual Exposure Impacts on Toddlers' Willingness to Taste Fruits and Vegetables," *Appetite* 53, no. 3 (October 2009): 450–53; Philippa Heath, Carmel Houston-Price, and Orla B. Kennedy, "Let's Look at Leeks! Picture Books Increase Toddlers' Willingness to Look at, Taste, and Consume Unfamiliar Vegetables," *Frontiers in Psychology* 5 (2014): 191; Philippa Heath, Carmel Houston-Price, and Orla B. Kennedy, "Increasing Food Familiarity without the Tears: A Role for Visual Exposure?" *Appetite* 57, no. 3 (2011): 832–38.

11 Jane Wardle and Lucy Cooke, "Genetic and Environmental Determinants of Children's Food Preferences," *British Journal of Nutrition* 99, no. S1 (2008): S15–S21.

12 Research published in *Appetite* shows that taking a step-by-step approach to taste testing helps kids learn to love a variety of vegetables over time: Marion Hetherington, Camille Schwartz, Jérôme Madrelle, F. Croden, Chandani Nekitsing, Carel M. J. L. Vereijken, and Hugo Weenen, "A Step-by-Step Introduction to Vegetables at the Beginning of Complementary Feeding: The Effects of Early and Repeated Exposure," *Appetite* 84 (January 2015): 280–90. In another study, researchers in the United Kingdom observed kids ages two to six years who participated in a program of parent-led taste testing of vegetables over two weeks' time. When parents gave children a taste of one veggie every day for fourteen days, the children exhibited a significant increase not only in willingness to eat that vegetable but also in liking it: Jane Wardle, Lucy J. Cooke, Edward Leigh Gibson, Manuela Sapochnik, Aubrey Sheiham, and Margaret Lawson, "Increasing Children's Acceptance of Vegetables: A Randomized Trial of Parent-Led Exposure," *Appetite* 40, no. 2 (May 2003): 155–62.

13 In one study, children as young as five were more willing to taste vegetables they previously rejected if they saw an adult obviously enjoying them: Laetitia Barthomeuf, Sylvie Droit-Volet, and Sylvie Rousset, "How Emotions Expressed by Adults' Faces Affect the Desire to Eat Liked and Disliked Foods in Children Compared to Adults," *British Journal of Developmental Psychology* 30, no. 2 (2011): 253–66.

14 Gertrud Sofie Hafstad, Dawit Shawel Abebe, Leila Torgersen, and Tilmann Von Soest, "Picky Eating in Preschool Children: The Predictive Role of the Child's Temperament and Mother's Negative Affectivity," *Eating Behaviors* 14, no. 3 (2013): 274–77.

15 Harriet Worobey, Kathleen Ostapkovich, Kristin Yudin, and John Worobey, "Trying Versus Liking Fruits and Vegetables: Correspondence Between Mothers and Preschoolers," *Ecology of Food and Nutrition* 49, no. 2 (2010): 87–97.

16 Ariun Ishdorj, Oral Capps, Maureen Storey, and Peter S. Murano, "Investigating the Relationship Between Food Pairings and Plate Waste from Elementary School Lunches," *Food and Nutrition Sciences* 6, no. 11 (2015): 1029–44.

17 Lucy J. Cooke, Lucy C. Chambers, Elizabeth V. Añez, and Jane Wardle, "Facilitating or Undermining? The Effect of Reward on Food Acceptance: A Narrative Review," *Appetite* 57, no. 2 (October 2011): 493–97.

18 Jane Anderson and Den Trumbull, "The Benefits of the Family Table," American College of Pediatricians, May 2014, acpeds.org/the-college-speaks/position-statements/parenting-issues/the-benefits-of-the-family-table; Marla E. Eisenberg, Rachel E. Olson, Dianne Neumark-Sztainer, Mary Story, and Linda H. Bearinger, "Correlations Between Family Meals and Psychosocial Well-Being Among Adolescents," *Archives of Pediatrics and Adolescent Medicine* 158, no. 8 (September 2004): 792.

19 Amber J. Hammons and Barbara H. Fiese, "Is Frequency of Shared Family Meals Related to the Nutritional Health of Children and Adolescents?" *Pedriatics* 127, no. 6 (June 2011), pediatrics.aappublications.org/content/127/6/e1565.

20 National Center on Addiction and Substance Abuse, "The Importance of Family Dinners VIII," September 2012, centeronaddiction.org/addiction-research/reports/importance-of-family-dinners-2012.

21 Catherine E. Snow and Diane Beals, "Mealtime Talk That Supports Literacy Development," *New Directions for Child and Adolescent Development* 111 (spring 2006): 51–66; Andrea Netten, Mienke Droop, and Ludo Verhoeven, "Predictors of Reading Literacy for First and Second Language Learners," *Reading and Writing* 24, no. 4 (April 2011): 413–25, europepmc.org/articles/PMC3058362.

22 Cynthia D. Klemmer, Tina M. Waliczek, and Jayne M. Zajicek, "Growing Minds: The Effect of a School Gardening Program on the Science Achievement of Elementary Students," *HortTechnology* 15, no. 3 (July–September 2005): 448–52, horttech.ashspublications.org/content/15/3/448.full.pdf+html.

23 "Growing Interest," Food & Brand Lab, Cornell University, 2017, foodpsychology.cornell.edu/discoveries/growing-interest.

24 Saint Louis University, "Children Eat More Fruits and Vegetables If They Are Homegrown," *ScienceDaily*, April 19, 2007, sciencedaily.com/releases/2007/04/070418163652.htm.

25 Nimali Fernando and Melanie Potock, "How Farmers Markets Can Help Foster Adventurous Eating," PBS Parents, April 14, 2016, pbs.org/parents/expert-tips-advice/2016/04/farmers-markets-can-help-foster-adventurous-eating.

26 Hammons and Fiese, "Frequency of Shared Family Meals."

Part One: Winter Vegetables

1 The American Academy of Pediatrics (AAP) recommends limiting juice as a beverage for kids ages one to three years to just 4 ounces (120 ml) per day. Kids between ages four and six should get no more than 6 ounces (175 ml) per day, and kids seven and up may have 8 ounces (235 ml) per day. The AAP strongly recommends no juice as a beverage for babies under the age of one due to the high sugar content. American Academy of Pediatrics, "Fruit Juice and Your Child's Diet," healthychildren.org/English/healthy-living/nutrition/Pages/Fruit-Juice-and-Your-Childs-Diet.aspx.

2 According to Mia McCloy, pediatric licensed occupational therapist.

Part Three: Summer Vegetables

1 "Bell Peppers," *The Old Farmer's Almanac*, almanac.com/plant/bell-peppers.

Appendix 1

1 American Speech-Language-Hearing Association, "Pediatric Dysphagia," ASHA Practice Portal, 2017, www.asha.org/PRPSpecificTopic.aspx?folderid=8589934965§ion=Incidence_and_Prevalence.

2 The lists of concerns about toddlers and school-age children are drawn from Nimali Fernando and Melanie Potock, *Raising a Healthy, Happy Eater: A Parent's Handbook—A Stage-by-Stage Guide to Setting Your Child on the Path to Adventurous Eating* (New York: The Experiment, 2015), 241–43.

3 Melanie Potock, "The Cooking Connection," *ASHA Leader*, April 2017, 46–52, leader.pubs.asha.org/article.aspx?articleid=2615521&resultClick=1.

4 Melanie Potock, "Our Perception of Taste: What's Sound Got to Do with It?" *ASHA Leader Blog*, March 4, 2014, blog.asha.org/2014/03/04/our-perception-of-taste-whats-sound-got-to-do-with-it.

5 Fernando and Potock, *Raising a Healthy, Happy Eater*, 20–21.

6 Valerie B. Duffy and Linda M. Bartoshuk, "Food Acceptance and Genetic Variation in Taste," *Journal of the American Dietetic Association* 100, no. 6 (2000): 647–55.

7 Martha R. Bajec, Gary J. Pickering, and Nancy Decourville, "Influence of Stimulus Temperature on Orosensory Perception and Variation with Taste Phenotype," *Chemosensory Perception* 5, nos. 3–4 (2012): 243–65; Mike Steinberger, "Is It Good to Be a Supertaster?" *Slate*, June 22, 2007, slate.com/articles/life/drink/2007/06/do_you_want_to_be_a_supertaster.html.

PHOTOGRAPHY CREDITS

INDEX

Note: Page references in *italics* indicate photographs.

ABOUT THE AUTHOR

Melanie Potock, MA, CCC-SLP, is an international speaker on the topics of parenting in the kitchen, picky eating, and raising kids to love healthy foods. With over twenty years' experience treating babies, toddlers, and school-age kids who struggle with eating, Melanie has shared her advice in major publications including *Parents* magazine and the *Huffington Post*. She has written five books, including *Responsive Feeding* and, with pediatrician Nimali Fernando as coauthor, the award-winning *Raising a Healthy, Happy Eater*. Melanie's website, melaniepotock.com, is a leading resource for professionals and parents seeking advice on how to introduce a variety of foods into a child's diet, how to avoid the chicken-nugget rut so prevalent in the United States, and how to bring the joy back to family mealtimes.